Instructor's Resource Manual

How to Study in College

SEVENTH EDITION

Walter Pauk

Director, Reading Research Center

Cornell University

Houghton Mifflin Company   Boston   New York

As part of Houghton Mifflin's ongoing commitment to the environment, this text has been printed on recycled paper.

Sponsoring Editor: Barbara A. Heinssen
Assistant Editor: Shani B. Fisher
Editorial Assistants: Cecilia Molinari and Sarah Godshall
Senior Manufacturing Coordinator: Priscilla Bailey
Marketing Manager: Stephanie Jones

Printed in the U.S.A.

ISBN: 0-618-04673-9

123456789-PAT-04 03 02 01 00

Contents

Preface   v

Part One   Multiple-Choice Questions   1

Answers to Multiple-Choice Questions   28

Part Two   Questions for Further Study and Discussion   29

Part Three   Supplementary Chapters   57

A Writing a Research Paper   59
B Studying Science   99
C Studying Foreign Languages   121
D Studying Literature   147

**Part Four   Using the "Roundtable Discussions"
Videotapes   161**

Preface

This *Instructor's Resource Manual* is designed to help instructors make better use of the seventh edition of *How to Study in College*. The manual contains numerous test questions for every chapter of the text, plus five supplementary chapters.

Part One, "Multiple-Choice Questions," contains ten multiple-choice questions for each chapter in the text. You can use these questions either as review aids or as quizzes. Answers are given at the end of the part.

Part Two, "Questions for Further Study and Discussion," is composed of more challenging supplemental questions for each text chapter. You may want to assign these questions as a follow-up to the questions presented in Part One or to those found in the "Have You Missed Something?" sections in the text. These open-ended questions are excellent aids for class discussion.

Part Three, "Supplementary Chapters," provides four chapters on special skills that may be of interest to your students: "Writing a Research Paper" (following this chapter is a selection titled "My First Research Paper" that functions as a review. Instructors report that students almost always comment, "I can now *visualize* how to put the entire writing process in action step by step."); "Studying Science," by Professor Kenneth Greisen of Cornell University; "Studying Foreign Languages"; and "Studying Literature." Each supplementary chapter ends with a summary in question-answer format, plus quiz questions and answers. You can photocopy these chapters and distribute them to your entire class or to selected students.

Part Four, "Using the 'Roundtable Discussions' Videotapes," is applicable for use in any course on study skills and techniques for success in college. The videotapes on *Study Strategies* cover the four primary proficiencies (note taking, reading, memory, and test taking). The *Life Skills* videotape addresses three areas that help to ensure success (goal setting, time management, and stress management).

I trust that this manual will prove helpful not only to students who strive to learn by systematic study but also to their instructors.

Walter Pauk

Part One

MULTIPLE-CHOICE QUESTIONS

1

CHAPTER 1 SETTING GOALS—A SELF-MANAGEMENT SKILL

1. A planned goal will help you to
   a. achieve success.
   b. keep focused.
   c. remain energized.
   d. do all the above.

2. Norman Vincent Peale believes that by *imaging* your goal, you
   a. visualize it with tremendous intensity.
   b. think about it often.
   c. dream of it, too.
   d. let daily events shape the direction.

3. The best way to become a success is by having
   a. a goal.
   b. a plan.
   c. a schedule of action.
   d. all of the above.

4. It helps to visualize your goal as a(n)
  a. accomplishment.
  b. serious task.
  c. destination.
  d. dream.

5. Your goal-plan should include
  a. only the major goal.
  b. both the major and minor goals.
  c. a day-by-day schedule.
  d. a year-by-year schedule.

6. When things go wrong,
  a. adopt a new plan.
  b. adjust and keep going.
  c. stay without a plan for a while.
  d. keep going on the original plan.

7. Putting your plan in action
  a. will come about naturally.
  b. should not be forced.
  c. is the spark that brings it to life.
  d. demands a step-by-step outline.

8. Procrastination is caused by
  a. fear of failure.
  b. fear of success.
  c. habitually putting things off.
  d. all the above.

9. You can overcome procrastination by
  a. analyzing the excuses.
  b. visualizing the first step to action.
  c. concentrating on successful outcomes.
  d. doing all the above.

10. Your chances of achieving your goal depend on your
  a. boiling it down to one written declarative sentence.
  b. setting a firm starting date.
  c. having an unshakable image of success.
  d. doing all the above.

CHAPTER 2   MANAGING YOUR TIME

1. You can gain extra time by
   a. finishing a job in less time.
   b. using blocks of time you usually waste.
   c. using a time schedule.
   d. doing all the above.

2. Pocket work may include
   a. a book.
   b. a photocopied article.
   c. 3×5 cards.
   d. all the above.

3. A time schedule should be considered a
   a. source of anxiety.
   b. written strategy.
   c. substitute for studying.
   d. last resort.

4. Time schedules make assignments and obligations more manageable by
   a. listing only the most important tasks.
   b. arranging them in order of priority.
   c. dividing them into blocks.
   d. automatically including recreation time.

5. The empty spaces in the master schedule grid represent
   a. required activities.
   b. food, sleep, and exercise.
   c. flexible time blocks.
   d. none of the above.

6. A task-based master schedule provides
   a. manageable subgoals.
   b. visual evidence of progress.
   c. positive feedback.
   d. all the above.

7. The daily schedule
   a. provides an adequate substitute for the master schedule.
   b. places all of your activities on a scheduling grid.
   c. puts the weekly schedule in a portable form.
   d. is helpful only for students with predictable schedules.

8. Use a list of things to do instead of a daily schedule when your time is
    a. short.
    b. unpredictable.
    c. occupied.
    d. flexible.

9. Studying before a recitation or discussion class
    a. is not recommended.
    b. provides a helpful warm-up.
    c. lets you fill in any gaps in your notes.
    d. results in interactive interference.

10. The Pareto Principle says that
    a. work expands to fit the time allotted.
    b. 80 percent of a list's importance lies in 20 percent of the list.
    c. study is twice as productive in the daytime as it is at night.
    d. productivity is tripled when tasks are divided up into blocks.

CHAPTER 3 MANAGING STRESS

1. Stress is the body's nonspecific response to
    a. demands.
    b. changes in temperature.
    c. high-pressure situations.
    d. physical exertion.

2. There is a strong connection between the way you breathe and
    a. your height and weight.
    b. the way you feel.
    c. your ability to remember.
    d. none of the above.

3. Self-esteem involves
    a. an ability to withstand criticism.
    b. your popularity with your peers.
    c. your assessment of your own value.
    d. a positive attitude toward others.

4. The first step in eliminating destructive thoughts is to
    a. think positive thoughts.
    b. accomplish something worthwhile.
    c. become aware of your thoughts.
    d. go to a quiet room and relax.

5. Taking control is primarily a matter of adjusting your
    a. schedule.
    b. attitude.
    c. priorities.
    d. desk chair.

6. You can build up your resistance to stress by
    a. improving your sleep.
    b. developing good eating habits.
    c. getting some exercise.
    d. doing all the above.

7. Lost sleep
    a. is cumulative; it adds up.
    b. can usually be made up on the weekend.
    c. should be remedied with naps.
    d. is seldom a problem for college students.

8. A recent report from the U.S. Department of Health and Human Services
    concluded that Americans
    a. eat too much fat.
    b. eat too much protein.
    c. don't eat enough carbohydrates.
    d. do all the above.

9. Exercise has been found to
    a. reduce stress.
    b. raise self-esteem.
    c. decrease depression.
    d. do all the above.

10. Most of the "cures" for procrastination
    a. work regardless of the cause.
    b. can be implemented instantly.
    c. require the help of others.
    d. are based on ancient principles.

CHAPTER 4   CONCENTRATING AND FOCUSING

1. You can improve the conditions for concentration by
    a. studying with music.
    b. deciding to concentrate.
    c. eliminating distractions.
    d. working out of doors.

2. A library normally provides
    a. a minimum of nonacademic distractions.
    b. a quiet atmosphere.
    c. sufficient lighting.
    d. all the above.

3. Reading or working in bed can
    a. make it difficult to work energetically.
    b. interfere with your ability to fall asleep.
    c. create a negative conditioning effect.
    d. do all the above.

4. The best light for studying is
    a. fluorescent light.
    b. bright, even, and steady.
    c. natural light.
    d. pale, shaded, and understated.

5. As you study, any nagging thoughts should be
    a. jotted on a worry pad.
    b. dealt with immediately.
    c. put out of your mind.
    d. considered study breaks.

6. An inventory list should include
    a. the titles of your textbooks.
    b. an outline of things to do.
    c. your most useful supplies.
    d. the cost of supplies for each of your courses.

7. Regular breaks can be used to
    a. defuse built-up distractions.
    b. enable you to have a snack.
    c. address a problem you've been avoiding.
    d. do all the above.

8. Csikszentmihalyi refers to intense concentration as
   a. balance.
   b. floating.
   c. flow.
   d. the zone.

9. If your skill level is high but the challenge of an assignment is low, you may become
   a. bored.
   b. anxious.
   c. tired.
   d. apathetic.

10. A concentration scoresheet is a tally of the times when your concentration has been
    a. strongest.
    b. broken.
    c. important.
    d. focused.

CHAPTER 5   FORGETTING AND REMEMBERING

1. Proponents of the retrieval theory believe that once an idea is thoroughly learned, it
   a. is impossible to forget.
   b. becomes a memory for life.
   c. may become lost or misfiled.
   d. may be hindered by emotions.

2. If you don't consciously learn new information,
   a. you'll pick it up subconsciously.
   b. you can't truly forget it.
   c. it will be forgotten almost immediately.
   d. none of the above.

3. G. A. Miller's "Magical Number Seven" refers to
   a. the limits of short-term memory.
   b. the world's most important facts.
   c. seven steps for memory building.
   d. none of the above.

4. The Silver Dollar System
   a. makes the process of selectivity easier.
   b. reduces the number of notes that you master.
   c. enables you to pinpoint important ideas.
   d. does all the above.

5. Information becomes more meaningful when it is
   a. arranged alphabetically.
   b. clustered or categorized.
   c. recalled, not recognized.
   d. rewritten or repeated.

6. No single activity is more important to strengthening memory than
   a. reciting.
   b. rereading.
   c. revising.
   d. none of the above.

7. In reciting, whether you're reading your notes or your text, you
   a. begin by extracting the main idea.
   b. arrive at a key word or question.
   c. demonstrate your knowledge out loud or on paper.
   d. do all the above.

8. Rereading
   a. is not the same as comprehending.
   b. can leave you with a false sense of confidence.
   c. won't make it clear where your weaknesses lie.
   d. all the above.

9. Consolidation supports the effectiveness of
   a. reflection.
   b. massed practice.
   c. distributed practice.
   d. rereading.

10. Lulls in learning are
   a. called memory plateaus.
   b. a natural part of consolidation.
   c. common to most people.
   d. all the above.

CHAPTER 6   BUILDING A PERMANENT VOCABULARY

1. An inadequate vocabulary may lead to difficulties in
   a. rationalizing.
   b. recognizing.
   c. conceptualizing.
   d. enterprising.

2. One valuable word-building tool that many of us neglect is
   a. a vocabulary.
   b. the dictionary.
   c. subvocalization.
   d. standardization.

3. Unlike genetic traits, your vocabulary is subject to
   a. personal specifications.
   b. traditional meanings.
   c. reverse discrimination.
   d. sudden mutation.

4. Words, like facts, are difficult to learn out of
   a. season.
   b. kindness.
   c. context.
   d. dictionaries.

5. Learning a word solely by context may sometimes provide you with
   a. only one of its meanings.
   b. an incorrect definition.
   c. a synonym for that word.
   d. all the above.

6. The core of a word is its
   a. definition.
   b. prefix.
   c. root.
   d. context.

7. The Frontier Vocabulary System is based on
   a. several expert word lists.
   b. Greek and Latin word roots.
   c. natural learning processes.
   d. an experiment done in space.

8. Only a few words beyond your own "frontier" have been
   a. defined.
   b. mastered.
   c. forgotten.
   d. useless.

9. The supply of frontier words is
   a. inexhaustible.
   b. ineligible.
   c. unmentionable.
   d. unforgettable.

10. Frontier words are often the kind that you encounter only in
    a. emergencies.
    b. speaking.
    c. writing.
    d. reading.

CHAPTER 7 IMPROVING YOUR READING SPEED AND COMPREHENSION

1. Speed-reading courses profess that the eyes can see a vast number of words in one
   a. movement.
   b. glance.
   c. reading.
   d. fixation.

2. A study at MIT found that in reading, the mind can attend to
   a. one letter at a time.
   b. one word at a time.
   c. four letters at a time.
   d. one sentence at a time.

3. There is strong evidence that vocalization is an essential part of
   a. reading.
   b. whispering.
   c. thinking.
   d. all the above.

4. The only effective way to increase your reading speed is to do so
    a. alternatively.
    b. naturally.
    c. occasionally.
    d. quietly.

5. Before you start reading a novel, it is important to
    a. scan the last page.
    b. create the proper mental set.
    c. compute your reading speed.
    d. consult the dictionary.

6. The intonation way makes use of the principle of
    a. vocalization.
    b. consolidation.
    c. comprehension.
    d. elevation.

7. In a precise vocabulary every word is learned as a
    a. magnet.
    b. rule.
    c. concept.
    d. synonym.

8. Edward Gibbon learned to use his old ideas as
    a. new ideas.
    b. magnetic centers.
    c. great rewards.
    d. cold facts.

9. The bulk of an expository paragraph is made up of
    a. new information.
    b. topic sentences.
    c. supporting sentences.
    d. old information.

10. Thomas Macaulay would summarize what he had read after every
    a. sentence.
    b. chapter.
    c. paragraph.
    d. page.

CHAPTER 8   UNDERSTANDING AND USING KEY CONCEPTS

1. The power of a question lies in its ability to
   a. promote concentration.
   b. alert you to words.
   c. stir the imagination.
   d. create a miniature miracle.

2. You can harness the power of questions by writing questions in
   a. the margins of textbooks.
   b. the margins of lecture notes.
   c. a notebook for research ideas.
   d. all the above.

3. Reflection converts information into
   a. long-term memory.
   b. wisdom.
   c. lasting learning.
   d. all the above.

4. Professor Bethe says that reflection promotes
   a. short-term memory.
   b. creativity.
   c. interest in science.
   d. test preparation.

5. According to Schopenhauer, knowledge should be
   a. accumulated.
   b. stored in long-term memory.
   c. thoroughly pondered.
   d. used in developing a philosophy.

6. One rewarding value of recognizing signal words is that they indicate
   a. tone of thought.
   b. ironical thought.
   c. satirical thought.
   d. direction of thought.

7. The main purpose of organizational patterns is to help
   a. emphasize persuasive speeches.
   b. students record the lecturer's ideas.
   c. organize a person's thoughts.
   d. newspapers report speeches more accurately.

8. Recognizing a lecturer's organizational pattern helps you to
    a. anticipate the lecturer's ideas.
    b. concentrate on what's being said.
    c. increase your self-confidence.
    d. all the above.

9. Such phrases as *on the other hand* are words of
    a. example.
    b. numeration.
    c. comparison.
    d. contrast.

10. When a principle is given first, then the facts, the pattern most likely is
    a. contrast.
    b. inductive.
    c. deductive.
    d. chronological.

CHAPTER 9   LISTENING TO TAKE GOOD NOTES

1. The prime requirement for effective listening is
    a. good notes.
    b. good questions.
    c. a positive attitude.
    d. a suspicious attitude.

2. Unlike listening, hearing is purely
    a. voluntary.
    b. mechanical.
    c. natural.
    d. additional.

3. A good way to begin concentrating is to
    a. anticipate the lecture.
    b. question the information.
    c. sharpen your pencil.
    d. listen without writing.

4. The average student, when tested immediately after a ten-minute lecture, remembers about
    a. 50 percent of the lecture.
    b. 25 percent of the lecture.
    c. 75 percent of the lecture.
    d. 10 percent of the lecture.

5. The average student, when tested forty-eight hours after a ten-minute lecture, remembers about
    a. 50 percent of the lecture.
    b. 25 percent of the lecture.
    c. 75 percent of the lecture.
    d. 10 percent of the lecture.

6. During a lecture period, you should never
    a. take notes.
    b. listen intently.
    c. read your textbook.
    d. ask questions.

7. During a lecture, it's a mistake to judge
    a. content, not delivery.
    b. delivery, not content.
    c. speed and accuracy.
    d. accuracy, not speed.

8. "Informed listening" means that the
    a. listener is being informed.
    b. speaker anticipates questions.
    c. listener can inform the speaker of any mistakes made.
    d. listener identifies the speaker's organizational patterns.

9. Some poor listeners
    a. quickly recognize speech patterns.
    b. get easily turned off by emotion-laden words.
    c. cause confusion in other listeners.
    d. require supplemental exercises.

10. Comprehensive listening occurs when the
    a. speaker is audible to the audience.
    b. listener encourages the speaker to fully articulate his or her message.
    c. speaker covers a broad range of topics.
    d. listener doesn't ask questions.

CHAPTER 10   TAKING GOOD NOTES

1. Modified printing is
    a. used by reporters.
    b. difficult to correct.
    c. slower than cursive.
    d. neater than cursive.

2. Try the two-page system if the lecturer is
    a. discussing science.
    b. talking too fast.
    c. stating main ideas.
    d. using big words.

3. If you use a tape recorder, you will
    a. learn a lot.
    b. waste time.
    c. review quickly.
    d. increase visual learning.

4. Begin reviewing a lecture
    a. after class.
    b. at home.
    c. at night.
    d. during class.

5. You should never takes notes in
    a. shorthand.
    b. longhand.
    c. abbreviated fashion.
    d. a language other than the lecturer's.

6. The type of notes you take depends on the nature of the
    a. school.
    b. notebook.
    c. material.
    d. questions.

7. Ideally, your notes should summarize the whole lecture and
    a. the last page of notes.
    b. the supporting details.
    c. each new idea.
    d. each page of notes.

8. Topic-explanation notes are useful for
    a. summaries.
    b. introductions.
    c. thematic or topical information.
    d. details.

9. In a lecture, abbreviatons should be used
    a. widely.
    b. almost entirely.
    c. only in science classes.
    d. sparingly.

10. The preferred method of taking lecture notes is using
    a. shorthand.
    b. the laptop computer.
    c. paper and pencil.
    d. courtroom shorthand devices.

CHAPTER 11 LEARNING FROM YOUR TEXTBOOKS

1. You should buy all your textbooks
    a. before you register for classes.
    b. right after you have registered.
    c. on the first day of classes.
    d. after the drop/add period.

2. Authors frequently drop their scholarly style in the
    a. end.
    b. introduction.
    c. preface.
    d. footnotes.

3. Introductions are usually
    a. lengthy.
    b. witty.
    c. self-conscious.
    d. packed with information.

4. Surveying can give you an instant
    a. intelligence.
    b. background.
    c. acceptance.
    d. assignment.

5. Advance organizers act as
   a. general contents.
   b. iron fillings.
   c. magnetic centers.
   d. learning theories.

6. Instead of turning headings into questions, some students prefer to
   a. ask general questions.
   b. look only for answers.
   c. supply new headings.
   d. write to the author.

7. Thinking, at its highest level, is
   a. opening your heart as well as your brain.
   b. reading only the world's greatest novels.
   c. using a large, unabridged dictionary.
   d. asking the right, relevant questions.

8. You get immediate feedback on how you're doing when you use
   a. consolidation.
   b. reinforcement.
   c. recitation.
   d. enjoyment.

9. The reflector is likely to
   a. follow the course outline.
   b. understand literal meaning only.
   c. understand facts in the sequential order of the textbook.
   d. be adventuresome and experimental.

10. "Advantageous learning" is learning that occurs when you
    a. use textbooks to your advantage.
    b. seek out your professor.
    c. take an extra step beyond mere memorizing.
    d. adhere to the course outline.

CHAPTER 12 NOTING WHAT'S IMPORTANT IN READINGS

1. Reading a textbook is a
   a. passive, relaxed activity.
   b. mental and physical activity.
   c. strictly mental activity.
   d. strictly physical activity.

2. To take notes you must
   a. consolidate.
   b. concentrate.
   c. reflect.
   d. review.

3. Concentration is on the path that leads to
   a. apprehension.
   b. comprehension.
   c. principles.
   d. underlining.

4. It is important to mark your textbook
   a. just before a quiz or exam.
   b. while you are reading a paragraph.
   c. only with scientific information.
   d. after you finish each paragraph.

5. Neatness in note taking takes more
   a. effort.
   b. ingenuity.
   c. intelligence.
   d. information.

6. It is important that your textbook marking be done
   a. consistently.
   b. frequently.
   c. deliberately.
   d. vehemently.

7. Double lines signify
   a. supporting materials.
   b. key transitions.
   c. main ideas.
   d. brief cues.

8. Underlining should be used
    a.   sparingly and effectively.
    b.   frequently and randomly.
    c.   entirely and completely.
    d.   marginally and neatly.

9. Edward Fox believes that notes are
    a.   an end in themselves.
    b.   a means to an end.
    c.   helpful in the end.
    d.   a never-ending source.

10. A great deal of "inside information" is provided in the
    a.   index.
    b.   chapters.
    c.   introduction.
    d.   preface.

CHAPTER 13   THINKING VISUALLY

1. One of the main functions of the brain's right side is to
    a.   analyze and interpret visual information.
    b.   serve as a connecting point for language and speech.
    c.   simplify information that the left side can't understand.
    d.   do all the above.

2. Thinking in pictures broadens your mind by
    a.   making use of both sides of your brain.
    b.   increasing emphasis on the brain's right side.
    c.   allowing for a balanced interpretation of information.
    d.   doing all the above.

3. The OPTIC system enables you to extract the message from
    a.   both words and pictures.
    b.   a variety of visuals.
    c.   line, circle, and bar graphs.
    d.   photographs and drawings.

4. Unlike the circle graph, bar and line graphs
    a.   compare parts to a whole.
    b.   incorporate percentages.
    c.   share the same basic function.
    d.   provide illustrations of data.

5. The popularity of the circle graph is due primarily to its
    a.   small size.
    b.   proportions.
    c.   simplicity.
    d.   slices.

6. Line graphs can be compared to
    a.   motion pictures.
    b.   snapshots.
    c.   long jumpers.
    d.   circle graphs.

7. Writing in pictures involves
    a.   turning a picture's message into a sentence or two.
    b.   reversing the process of reading in pictures.
    c.   expanding your overall understanding.
    d.   understanding the language of graphs.

8. Single concepts in a concept map can be used as cues for
    a.   larger maps.
    b.   recitation.
    c.   selectivity.
    d.   information.

9. Summary maps, like summary paragraphs,
    a.   are written at the bottom of each note sheet.
    b.   contain highly detailed information.
    c.   cover only the most important ideas.
    d.   are usually several pages long.

10. In writing a paper or preparing an oral report, you can use a concept map as
    a.   an outline.
    b.   a guide for research.
    c.   a planning strategy.
    d.   all the above.

CHAPTER 14   MANAGING TEST ANXIETY

1. The remedy for test anxiety is
   a. preparation.
   b. relaxation.
   c. avoidance.
   d. perseverance

2. Exam preparation should begin
   a. at midterm.
   b. on the first day of class.
   c. during the second week of class.
   d. during finals week.

3. The most efficient way of transferring information from short-term memory to long-term memory is by
   a. tape-recording lectures.
   b. studying in groups.
   c. taking quizzes throughout the term.
   d. taking notes.

4. The home-stretch schedule
   a. uses the same grid as the master schedule.
   b. covers the week before exam week.
   c. includes all pre-exam obligations.
   d. does all the above.

5. Summary sheets are
   a. pages that contain a brief synopsis of a textbook chapter.
   b. a highly concentrated version of your notes.
   c. composed of the top idea from each page of your notes.
   d. useful only for essay exams.

6. Preparing summary sheets enables you to
   a. review and add to your notes.
   b. produce a super-concentrated version of your notes.
   c. categorize information so it is easier to remember.
   d. do all the above.

7. The way to make cramming successful is by
   a. cramming systematically.
   b. limiting what you try to learn.
   c. spending your time reciting instead of rereading.
   d. doing all the above.

8. One obvious but overlooked method of finding out about an exam is
   a. asking the instructor directly.
   b. reading a testing manual.
   c. studying your textbook carefully.
   d. checking with your classmates.

9. Test-anxious students often sabotage their efforts by
   a. cultivating false confidence.
   b. checking through old exams.
   c. relying too heavily on recitation.
   d. mentally preparing for failure.

10. During an exam, you can sometimes calm yourself down by taking
    a. the suggestion of a close friend or adviser.
    b. a series of deep, slow breaths.
    c. a two-minute break.
    d. a pillow or cushion to your desk.

CHAPTER 15   MASTERING OBJECTIVE TESTS

1. Aside from understanding the questions, mastering an objective test involves
   a. choosing an effective study method.
   b. moving systematically through the test.
   c. learning strategies for specific question types.
   d. all the above.

2. Choosing the correct answer in a multiple-choice question involves
   a. mentally connecting the options to the stem.
   b. turning each option into a true-false statement.
   c. placing the question in a variety of formats.
   d. none of the above.

3. Matching quickly can
   a. lead to a chain reaction of mistakes.
   b. save you time.
   c. improve your odds.
   d. eliminate the need for guessing.

4. The safest way to prepare for an objective test is by
   a. determining the format of the test as soon as possible.
   b. going over tests from previous terms.
   c. studying to the point of recall.
   d. none of the above.

5. Study "switch hitting" involves
   a. mastering your notes in both directions.
   b. using the right side of the brain.
   c. recalling important information instantly.
   d. none of the above.

6. Qualifiers complicate a simple statement or option by adding a
   a. dimension.
   b. negative.
   c. qualification.
   d. distinction.

7. Although their formats may vary, all objective questions
   a. follow the rules of grammar.
   b. have only one possible answer.
   c. focus on details instead of themes.
   d. require recall instead of recognition.

8. On an exam question, you should make an intelligent guess
   a. even if there's a penalty for incorrect answers.
   b. if you're still stumped on your third pass through the test.
   c. instead of leaving it blank.
   d. all the above.

9. One way to gain a new perspective on a difficult multiple-choice question is by using
   a. the Spider technique.
   b. the true-false technique.
   c. grammatical clues.
   d. marginal notes.

10. In general, the length of the blank in a sentence-completion question
    a. increases for more difficult questions.
    b. indicates the length of the correct answer.
    c. varies depending on its placement in the sentence.
    d. has no bearing on the appropriate answer.

CHAPTER 16   TACKLING ESSAY TESTS

1. Unlike objective questions, essay questions require
    a.   systematic study.
    b.   an ability to recognize correct information.
    c.   accurate recollection of facts and ideas.
    d.   all the above.

2. Relevant thoughts that occur to you before you begin an essay exam
    should be
    a.   put out of your mind.
    b.   jotted down on the back of your exam sheet.
    c.   saved so they won't be forgotten.
    d.   all the above.

3. The directions for an essay exam will often establish
    a.   the length of your answers and the time you're allotted.
    b.   the approach you should take.
    c.   the number of questions you should answer.
    d.   all the above.

4. If time is running out, any unfinished essays should be
    a.   outlined.
    b.   erased.
    c.   finished quickly.
    d.   left incomplete.

5. You should begin writing your essay exam by answering the
    a.   first question.
    b.   last question.
    c.   easiest question.
    d.   most difficult question.

6. You can ensure that your essay will get to the point by
    a.   leaving off the introduction.
    b.   putting your answer at the very beginning.
    c.   avoiding rambling writing.
    d.   doing all the above.

7. The thought flow of your essay will be easier to follow if you
    a.   begin with a detailed introduction.
    b.   write your essay in outline format.
    c.   use a recognizable organizational pattern.
    d.   write in pencil instead of in pen.

8. The most straightforward way of organizing your essay is by using the
   a. decreasing-importance pattern.
   b. increasing-importance pattern.
   c. pattern that your instructor prefers.
   d. same idea to open each paragraph.

9. Your essay should end with a
   a. new point.
   b. summary.
   c. question.
   d. statistic.

10. The evidence in your essay should be
    a. factual
    b. footnoted.
    c. opinionated.
    d. entertaining.

CHAPTER 17   STUDYING MATHEMATICS

1. College work in mathematics begins with
   a. algebra.
   b. arithmetic.
   c. trigonometry.
   d. calculus.

2. One of the best things to do if you have a weak math background is to
   a. start all over again.
   b. see a counselor.
   c. try solving puzzles.
   d. spot review.

3. When you take notes in a math class, you should
   a. pay close attention to the details.
   b. record only the examples.
   c. record as much of the lecture as possible.
   d. determine how to attack particular kinds of problems.

4. If a particular computation in your textbook stumps you, you should
   a. get another textbook.
   b. skim other problems like it to understand the theory.
   c. work through it until you understand it.
   d. first consult your instructor.

5. Studying for exams is likely to be most productive if you
   a. memorize formulas only.
   b. reread your textbook.
   c. review problems you have had in assignments.
   d. recopy your notes.

6. A component of problem solving not to be undertaken in the first stage of your work on a problem is
   a. calculating.
   b. noting.
   c. sorting.
   d. analyzing.

7. A calculator will
   a. inhibit you.
   b. teach you bad habits.
   c. remove the tedium from calculations.
   d. decrease your motivation for problem solving.

8. Math instructors often assign nonroutine problems primarily to test your
   a. endurance.
   b. computations.
   c. longevity.
   d. creativity.

9. Most students in their work on mathematics rely too much on their
   a. intuition.
   b. expertise.
   c. memory.
   d. numerical skills.

10. Developing good study habits in mathematics is important
   a. mainly for what you learn about nonmathematical subjects.
   b. only if you're likely to become a math or sciences major.
   c. because there won't always be an instructor or textbook around.
   d. only if you feel you can't learn the material on your own.

CHAPTER 18 LEARNING WITH THE COMPUTER

1. An introductory course in computer applications is not likely to require that you learn
    a. spreadsheet accounting.
    b. database management.
    c. computer programming.
    d. word processing.

2. *Computer literacy* refers to
    a. the ability to decipher computer manuals.
    b. how the computer decodes information.
    c. material displayed on the screen.
    d. a working understanding of word processing and of manipulating information.

3. *Software* refers to
    a. instructions that direct the computer.
    b. the material that floppy disks are made of.
    c. the soft, not the hard, copy.
    d. the flow of information through the computer's circuits.

4. It is important, when determining your computer requirements, to
    a. read as many computer books from the bookstore as you can.
    b. consider how a computer course will fit into your long-term plan of study.
    c. take as many courses as you can.
    d. think about the benefits of a computer programming course.

5. The highest quality of print comes from a
    a. laser printer.
    b. daisy wheel printer.
    c. dot matrix printer.
    d. high-quality dot matrix printer.

6. A helpful feature of many word-processing programs is called the
    a. modem.
    b. field.
    c. filing cabinet.
    d. spelling checker.

7. An electronic schedule allows you to
    a. know when the computer will be on-line.
    b. create lists of your deadlines and target dates.
    c. revise information in an accounting program.
    d. decide how your next document will be outputed.

8. Using a spreadsheet program allows you to store
   a. files, lists, and packages.
   b. programs, disks, and letters.
   c. sheets, models, and diskettes.
   d. numbers, words, and formulas.

9. Most databases hold
   a. a few hundred million pieces of information.
   b. a million or so pieces of information.
   c. a few hundred or a few thousand pieces of information.
   d. ten large pieces of information.

10. In-library bibliographic searches won't allow you to
    a. access your library's holdings.
    b. search the files of an off-campus service.
    c. perform quick searches.
    d. refine your search.

ANSWERS TO MULTIPLE-CHOICE QUESTIONS

	Goals	Time	Stress	Concentration	Forgetting	Vocabulary	Reading	Key Concepts	Listening	Note Taking	Textbooks	Noting Text	Thinking Visually	Test Anxiety	Objective Tests	Essay Tests	Mathematics	Computer
										Chapter								
Question	1	2	3	4	5	6	7	8	9	10	11	12	13	14	15	16	17	18
1	d	d	a	c	c	c	d	a	c	d	b	b	a	a	d	c	b	c
2	a	d	b	d	c	b	b	d	b	b	c	b	d	b	a	d	d	d
3	d	b	c	d	a	d	d	c	a	b	d	b	b	d	a	d	d	a
4	c	c	c	b	d	c	b	c	a	a	b	d	c	d	c	a	c	b
5	b	c	b	a	b	d	b	d	b	a	c	a	c	b	a	c	c	a
6	b	d	d	c	a	c	a	d	c	c	a	a	a	d	c	d	a	d
7	c	d	a	d	d	c	c	b	b	d	d	c	b	d	a	c	c	b
8	d	b	d	c	d	b	b	d	d	c	c	a	b	a	b	a	d	d
9	d	b	d	a	c	a	c	d	b	b	d	b	c	d	b	b	c	c
10	d	b	a	b	d	d	d	c	b	c	c	d	d	b	d	a	c	b

2

Part Two

QUESTIONS FOR FURTHER STUDY AND DISCUSSION

CHAPTER 1 SETTING GOALS—A SELF-MANAGEMENT SKILL

1. Why is a focus necessary in carrying out a goal?

Shaping Your Future Through Goals

2. Why is Norman Vincent Peale's concept of *imaging* such a powerful force?

What Is the Best Way to Become a Success?

3. Explain the meaning of the special GPA.

A Famous Goal, Plan, and Action

4. What does the episode of the astronauts landing on the moon illustrate?

All About Goals

5. What quality does having a goal impart?
6. Why do people equate goals with destinations?
7. Why have minor goals, too?
8. How do you decide on a goal?
9. How large should a major goal be?
10. What should you do with your goal once you've chosen it?
11. Are you stuck with a goal until you reach it?
12. What is a plan?
13. How can you choose the most efficient plan?
14. How can you tell whether you have an efficient plan?
15. Can you be sure you've chosen the right goal?
16. Does a single plan work for every goal? Explain.
17. How can you determine the best plan to achieve your personal goal?
18. Is a good plan guaranteed to work?
19. What do we mean by "taking action on a goal"?
20. What prevents people from taking action?
21. What causes procrastination?
22. How can you overcome procrastination?
23. Why is it important to have a written goal?
24. Why is it important to read your goal every day?
25. What happens when you visualize your goal?

CHAPTER 2   MANAGING YOUR TIME

1. What did the Fordham study reveal about the amount of "free time" that freshmen had?
2. How can you gain extra time?

Saving Time

3. How can you put your time to better use?
4. What is the purpose of a daily activities log?
5. How can you use what you've learned from the activities log?
6. What is Parkinson's Law?
7. What is the advantage of taking time out from your work?

8. How can you use a notepad to save time?

9. How can you make the most of hidden time?

10. What is pocket work? What is its purpose?

11. In what situations is your mind "free"?

12. How can audiocassettes help you make the most of hidden time?

13. What is "spare-time" thinking?

14. How can you enlist your subconscious to make the most of hidden time?

Using Time Schedules

15. What is the role of a time schedule?

16. What are the schedules that make up the three-part scheduling plan?

17. How will a full-time job or other time-consuming outside activity affect the principles that underlie three-part scheduling?

18. What is the difference among the master, weekly, and daily schedules?

19. What is the benefit of scheduling your time in blocks?

20. What is the prime studying time for most people?

21. When is the best time to study for recitation classes?

22. When is the best time to study for lecture classes?

23. Why and how should your schedule incorporate nonacademic activities?

24. What goes in the master schedule boxes?

25. How does the weekly schedule differ from the master schedule?

26. Under what circumstances would you need to adopt traditional schedules?

27. How does the task-based master schedule make assignments seem easier?

28. When is the use of an assignment-oriented weekly schedule beneficial?

29. Under what circumstances is using a list of things to do preferable to using a daily schedule?

30. What is the Pareto Principle?

CHAPTER 3 MANAGING STRESS

1. What is stress?

2. What is the two-sided potential of stress?

Developing a Positive Mental Attitude

3. What influences your response to stress?
4. What did James and Lange suggest in relation to stress?
5. How can you systematically improve your attitude?
6. What does relaxation entail?
7. What effect does breathing have on your emotions?
8. What is the count-of-three method?
9. What is progressive muscle relaxation?
10. What is self-esteem?
11. How can you improve your self-esteem?
12. How can past success aid your solution of present problems?
13. How does your attitude affect your sense of control?

Following a Healthy Physical Routine

14. How can you increase your resistance to stress?
15. What are the potential effects of a lack of sleep?
16. How does stress affect the need for sleep?
17. What are circadian rhythms?
18. What is the relationship, in terms of productivity, between daytime and nighttime hours?
19. What effect does napping have on your ability to learn?
20. Why is breakfast so important?
21. What basic guidelines do nutritionists agree upon?
22. What does mealtime provide in addition to nutrients?
23. What role does protein play in your body's upkeep?
24. What psychological benefit can protein provide?
25. What is the nutritional function of fat?
26. Why is excess fat more dangerous than excess protein?
27. What are the drawbacks of simple carbohydrates?
28. What are the advantages of exercise?
29. How often should you exercise?
30. What is aerobic exercise, and what is its greatest benefit?
31. In what way is exercise an example of good stress?

Reducing Stressors

32. How can you reduce the number of stressors you encounter?
33. What are some of the causes of procrastination?
34. What are some ways of fighting procrastination?

CHAPTER 4 CONCENTRATING AND FOCUSING

1. What is concentration?

Understanding What Concentration Means

2. What makes concentration difficult to achieve?
3. How can you achieve concentration if you can't seek it directly?

Eliminating Distractions

4. What are external distractions?
5. What are internal distractions?
6. How can you reduce external distractions?
7. What is the right study environment?
8. What is the advantage of studying in the library?
9. What is the conditioning effect between students and their desks?
10. Why is reading or working in bed not a good idea?
11. How can you ensure a proper study environment?
12. How can you minimize visual distractions?
13. How can you eliminate noise?
14. Why is music considered noise?
15. What effect does lighting have on concentration?
16. How can you obtain a steady light source?
17. What is the Spider technique?
18. How does the chair you choose affect your concentration?
19. What is the value of a bookstand?

20. Why is it helpful to keep your work area well equipped?
21. What is a concentration scoresheet?
22. How does a worry pad help you handle the problem of internal distractions?

Adopting Strategies That Encourage Concentration

23. What strategies can you apply that will encourage concentration?
24. What should you include in an inventory list?
25. What are the advantages of taking breaks?
26. How do your level of skill and your level of interest influence concentration?
27. What happens when an assignment's challenge exceeds your skill level?
28. What happens when your skill level is high but an assignment is not challenging?
29. What happens when both the challenge and the skill level are low?
30. What are four strategies for increasing your skills and interest level?

CHAPTER 5   FORGETTING AND REMEMBERING

Understanding How We Forget

1. Why is spoken information more difficult to remember than written information?
2. What explanations do experts offer for the causes of forgetfulness?

Making an Effort to Remember

3. What is pseudo-forgetting?
4. What effect does motivation have on memory?
5. What are three ways you can strengthen your intention to remember?
6. How can you put motivated forgetting to positive use?

Controlling the Number and Form of Your Memories

7. What is the limit in size of each item you try to remember?
8. What is the purpose of the Silver Dollar System?
9. What is the significance of ideas marked with $?

Strengthening Memories

10. What are two ways of strengthening memories?
11. What is a memory network?
12. How do you ensure that a link is made between new memories and old memories?
13. What are two ways of making logical connections to your memory network?
14. What is the principle behind basic background?
15. What are three ways of building your basic background?
16. Why does making pictures help to reinforce your memory?
17. What are mnemonic devices?
18. What is a keyword mnemonic?
19. Name and describe the two steps used in using keyword mnemonics.
20. What is the verbal step of the keyword mnemonic?
21. What is the source for the letters that make up a create-a-word mnemonic?
22. How do the steps for create-a-word and create-a-sentence mnemonics differ?
23. Which is easier to devise—create-a-word or create-a-sentence mnemonics?
24. What are some drawbacks of the peg system?
25. What is the single most important activity for strengthening memory?
26. What is the best method of reciting?
27. What is the procedure for traditional reciting?
28. What are some common complaints or concerns about reciting?
29. What are the three basic steps of reciting?
30. Contrast the memory principle used in mastering material using key words versus the principle used in mastering material using questions.
31. How does reciting strengthen your memory?
32. What sort of psychological benefit does reciting provide?

Allowing Time for Memories to Consolidate

33. How helpful is rereading compared with reciting?
34. What is distributed practice, and what are some of its advantages?
35. In what situations is massed practice superior to distributed practice?
36. What are memory plateaus?

CHAPTER 6   BUILDING A PERMANENT VOCABULARY

1. Why is a good vocabulary related to success?

Using a Dictionary

2. What is recommended as the only sure way to get a powerful vocabulary?
3. Briefly describe the 3 × 5 card system. What information would you put on each side of the cards?
4. What are the steps in studying your vocabulary cards?
5. What is the major advantage of the 3 × 5 card system?
6. What is the main value in reading a pocket dictionary?
7. Why should you use an abridged dictionary?
8. What is the advantage of an unabridged dictionary?
9. What are the three limitations of using context to get the meaning of new words?
10. What is a word root? What does it do?
11. What is a prefix? What does it do? Where is it placed in relation to a word?

Becoming Interested in the Origin of Words

12. List four ingredients necessary to make vocabulary building a productive adventure.

13. Find the origins of the following words:
     a. maverick
     b. boycott
     c. Yankee
     d. gerrymander
     e. salary

Using the Frontier Vocabulary System

14. What are the four characteristics of natural learning processes?
15. What are the principles of learning new words?
16. What are the three zones in the Frontier System?
17. Where does the most learning take place? Why?
18. List the four steps in finding your own frontier words.
19. How does the Frontier System relate to the note-card system?

Testing Your Vocabulary

20. How should you work with your new words from classes and textbooks?

CHAPTER 7   IMPROVING YOUR READING SPEED AND COMPREHENSION

1. What is the only way to obtain high comprehension and complete retention?

Eye Movements During Reading

2. What is the basic premise of speed-reading?
3. What is a fixation?
4. How many words, on average, can the eye see during a fixation?
5. How many usable letters does the eye take in during each fixation?
6. What is the pattern of these letters?
7. According to Richard Feinberg, how many letters are seen with 100 percent sharpness? How does this sharpness decrease as the letters get farther away from the fixation point?

How Much the Mind Can See

8. What was the conclusion of the MIT researchers about perception?
9. Why do readers get the impression that they are seeing more than one word at a time?
10. What is the final objection cited to speed-reading?

Vocalization While Reading

11. What are the four types of vocalizers?
12. Is the elimination of vocalization desirable? Why or why not?
13. What is subvocalization?
14. Why is it true that we all subvocalize?
15. What does Ake Edfelt say about subvocalization?
16. What did Thorndike say about reading? How does this relate to psychologists' theories of thinking?

A Natural Way to Read Faster

17. What is the only effective way to increase reading speed?
18. Is reading at a faster speed appropriate when you read a textbook?
19. When should you use the faster reading technique?
20. What are the five things to do as you practice faster reading? Name and describe each one.
21. Why should you not try to calculate your words-per-minute speed?
22. How should you read the first book?
23. How should you read books two through five?
24. What happens after the sixth book?
25. What should you do if you lose interest in a book?

The Intonation Way

26. What is intonation?
27. Do you need to say the words out loud in the intonation system?
28. What is meant by "your inner voice"?
29. Why should you first start reading aloud?

The Vocabulary Way

30. What is meant by learning each word as a concept?

31. Why should you learn each word as a concept?

The Background Way

32. What does Donald Ausubel say is the most important prerequisite for learning?

33. Why is this background so important?

Edward Gibbon's Way

34. Who was Edward Gibbon?

35. What did Gibbon do before reading a new book?

36. Why is Gibbon's system so successful? List the learning principles involved.

The Paragraph Way

37. What is the function of the topic sentence?

38. What are the functions of supporting sentences?

39. What is the function of the concluding sentence?

40. What are the three types of paragraphs? What is the purpose of each?

The Page-at-a-Time Way

41. Why did Macaulay develop the Page-at-a-Time system?

42. How is the system used?

Daniel Webster's Way

43. What did Webster do before reading a book?

44. What three lists did he make after doing this preliminary work?

45. How did these lists help him comprehend what he was reading?

The Skimming Way

46. When you are skimming for specific information, how can you be sure not to overlook the word or fact that you are searching for?

47. What is the difference between looking for clues and looking for specific information?

48. How can you use skimming to get the gist of a book or article?

49. Why should you get an overview of a book or chapter before you read?

50. How would you use skimming to help you get an overview?

51. When skimming for a review, what should you do every so often to check your comprehension?

52. Why should you overview after reading a chapter?

CHAPTER 8   UNDERSTANDING AND USING KEY CONCEPTS

1. What are the five key concepts?

Questions: Become Your Own Teacher

2. How do self-formulated questions help you to become your own teacher?

The Power of Questions

3. How did Socrates use questions?

4. Why is concentration so hard to maintain?

Questions Promote Alertness

5. How do questions promote alertness?

Harnessing the Power of Questions

6. How can you make practical use of questions?

The Science of Recitation

7.   How does recitation enhance memory?
8.   What's the most productive way to use recitation? Why?
9.   What's the difference between recognition and recall?

Gaining Mastery and Wisdom Through Reflection

10.   What is reflection?
11.   What does Professor Hans Bethe say about reflection?
12.   What analogy does Arthur Schopenhauer use to explain the value of reflection?
13.   What specific questions can you ask to jump-start the process of reflection?

Recognizing and Using Signal Words

14.   What would the phrase *on the other hand* usually indicate?
15.   What would the phrase *in other words* usually indicate?

Recognizing and Using Organizational Patterns

16.   How can the recognition of an organizational pattern help you in reading a textbook?
17.   In a lecture in history, if the lecturer says, "Let's take it from the beginning," what pattern would you anticipate?

CHAPTER 9   LISTENING TO TAKE GOOD NOTES

Hearing Versus Listening

1.   How do hearing and listening differ?
2.   What activities are involved in the process of listening?
3.   What is concentration? How can you initiate it?
4.   What role does active listening play in remembering?

Keys to Effective Listening

5. What strategies are recommended for improving listening?

6. How can you develop a genuine internal interest in classes that you don't find interesting?

7. What does approaching lectures with a "humane" attitude refer to?

8. How should you respond to the ideas of lecturers when they are different or even contrary to your own? Why should you do this?

9. What should you listen for when taking notes? Why is this important?

10. What patterns do speakers often use to organize their ideas? How do they differ?

11. What characteristics does a good listener display in the classroom?

12. What is the best way to resist distractions during class?

13. Can listening skills be exercised? If so, how?

14. What is the value of keeping an open mind while listening?

15. What can you do as a listener to keep your mind from wandering?

16. In what way is overreacting likely to hinder effective listening? What is the best way to avoid overreacting?

17. How can effective listeners reduce the impact of words or phrases that they find emotionally loaded?

Comprehensive Listening

18. What is comprehensive listening?

19. Why is comprehensive listening a two-way street?

20. How do both speaker and listener benefit from questions asked by the listener?

21. What is the best way to ask a speaker for clarification when you are too confused to know exactly what to ask?

22. How should you answer questions posed by the instructor during a lecture?

The Listening Attitude

23. What is the most important key to effective listening? In what way is this key likely to affect listening success?

CHAPTER 10   TAKING GOOD NOTES

The Importance of Notes

1. Forgetting is described as instant and massive. How is this claim supported?
2. Why is taking notes the only sure way to overcome forgetting?

Tips and Tactics

3. What are telegraphic sentences? What advantages do they offer note takers?
4. What style of note taking is recommended for taking neat and efficient notes?
5. How does the "two-page" system for taking notes differ from the Cornell note-taking system? When should the two-page system be used?
6. Why is it unwise to record lectures on tape instead of taking notes?
7. What is the disadvantage of taking shorthand notes?
8. Why should you avoid typing notes?
9. Why should you identify signal words and phrases during a lecture?
10. Why should you pay particularly close attention to the final minutes of a lecture?
11. What is the best way to ensure deep cognitive processing of lecture material?
12. What are "ice-cold" notes? How can they be avoided?
13. What do you believe are the five most important "do's" of note taking? Why are they important?
14. What would you identify as the two biggest "don'ts" of note taking? Why are they important?

The Cornell Note-Taking System

15. What is the general format for taking notes in the Cornell System?
16. What six steps does the Cornell System use to promote effective learning?
17. What is the difference between cue columns and question columns in the Cornell System? How are appropriate cues or questions developed?

18. What is the purpose of recitation? How should you go about reciting from lecture notes?
19. Why is reflection a powerful learning tool?
20. What type of review is best for the most effective learning to occur?
21. What are the advantages to writing summaries of your notes? Where can summaries be used in the Cornell System?

Types of Notes

22. The Cornell format can make use of what four types of notes?
23. What type of combined note-taking format is effective when lectures follow and amplify material in the textbook?

Abbreviations and Symbols

24. How should abbreviations and symbols be introduced into your note taking? Which of the examples in the abbreviations and symbols list look particularly useful to you? Why?

CHAPTER 11   LEARNING FROM YOUR TEXTBOOKS

Getting Acquainted with Your Textbooks

1. Why should you buy your texts before the semester starts?
2. Which specific portions of the texts you purchase should you read before the semester starts? Why?
3. What specific information can be found in the preface?
4. What specific information did you find in the preface to *How to Study in College*?
5. List four good reasons for reading introductions.

The SQ3R Method

6. What are the five steps in the SQ3R method?
7. What is the purpose of the survey step?

8. What is the purpose of the question step?
9. What is your purpose when you read?
10. How do you recite?
11. How should you review?

The Questions-in-the-Margin System

12. Why should you survey? List the four reasons stated for the importance of surveying.
13. What are advance organizers?
14. List the major points to guide your surveying.
15. What is the main reason that asking questions works?
16. What should you always make a point to do when you ask questions?
17. What is the most crucial step in the process of studying a textbook?
18. Should you ever go beyond a problem paragraph? If so, when and why?
19. At the end of each paragraph, what should you ask yourself?
20. What should you do after you read and summarize a paragraph? Why?
21. When you encounter unfamiliar words in your text, what three things should you do to learn them?
22. When do you write the question in the margin?
23. What do you do after writing the question?
24. Why should you underline as little as possible?
25. How do you use the questions in the margin to review the chapter?
26. Why recite aloud?
27. What will be the major academic problem for most students?
28. What five things does reciting do for you?
29. Why is visualizing helpful when reciting?
30. How should you end your study session?
31. What is the purpose of this session?
32. What should you look for when you review (immediately or later)?
33. What is the best time for a fast review of the text?
34. What should you do to become curious about the facts and ideas you have learned?
35. What is meant by *advantageous learning*?
36. Why is reflecting so important in the learning process?

CHAPTER 12 NOTING WHAT'S IMPORTANT IN READINGS

1.   What are the two reasons given for marking your texts?

The Standard System

2.   When should you begin marking your text?
3.   Why should you wait until this time?
4.   What do you want to highlight during your review?
5.   Why is it important to use your own words?
6.   How will cross-referencing help?
7.   How can overmarking defeat the purpose of marking the text?

The Questions-in-the-Margin System

8.   List the four steps in the Questions-in-the-Margin System.
9.   How does the Questions-in-the-Margin System differ from the Standard System?
10. What kinds of questions should you make up?

The Separate Notes System

11. What is the Cornell note-taking system?
12. When should you make notes?
13. Why should you use full sentences?
14. Why did Edward W. Fox say that notes taken in paragraph form are the best?

Reading and Taking Notes on Supplemental Material

15. List four reasons a teacher might assign supplemental readings.
16. Why is it important to determine why the reading was assigned?
17. What are the three parts of the book you must be certain to read?
18. What types of questions should you be ready to answer about supplemental readings?

19. What type of note taking on supplemental material is best?

Using Your Notes

20. Why should you read over your notes?
21. How should you study your written notes?
22. Is this method different from that of studying your lecture notes?
23. What is the best way to prepare for an examination?

CHAPTER 13   THINKING VISUALLY

1. What is visual thinking?

Using Your Whole Brain

2. What are the chief functions of each of the brain's hemispheres?
3. How does thinking in pictures affect the brain?
4. Why will thinking in pictures broaden your mind and improve your understanding?
5. What effect does whole-brain thinking have on memory?
6. What is "dual coding"?

Extracting Meaning from Pictures

7. How does reading a paragraph compare with reading a visual?
8. What is the meaning of the five letters that make up the acronym OPTIC?
9. What types of graphs are you most likely to encounter?
10. What is the purpose of a circle graph?
11. What accounts for the popularity of the circle graph?
12. What is the purpose of bar and line graphs?
13. What are variables?
14. Why are certain variables referred to as independent?
15. What are dependent variables?
16. How do bar and line graphs differ?
17. How are bar and line graphs like snapshots and movies?

Expanding Understanding with Graphics

18. How do you write in pictures?
19. How do you draw pictures of abstract ideas?
20. What is the purpose of concept maps?
21. How do you create a concept map?
22. What is the simplest method for mastering a concept map?
23. How can the concepts in a concept map be used for recitation?
24. How will adding to a concept map help you master it?
25. What is the advantage of redrawing your concept map?
26. How can maps be used as summaries?
27. What concepts should you include in a summary map?
28. How does a summary map compare with a summary paragraph?
29. What role can a concept map play in the planning of a paper or oral report?
30. What advantage does a concept map have over a traditional outline?

CHAPTER 14   MANAGING TEST ANXIETY

1. What is the simple cure for test anxiety?

Preparing Yourself Academically

2. What does academic preparation entail?
3. How do you get an early start on a course?
4. What is the advantage of looking through your textbook before the course has begun?
5. What can the syllabus tell you that will aid your preparation?
6. When should you familiarize yourself with the campus tutoring service?
7. When should your exam preparation begin?
8. Why should you stay on top of your coursework?
9. Why is taking notes important in test preparation?
10. What should you do to organize yourself for an upcoming test?
11. What is the point of the home-stretch schedule?
12. What's the best way of organizing your notes before an exam?
13. How can you reduce your notes to a set of summary sheets?

14. What is the value of creating summary sheets?

15. How do you make up a set of regular summary sheets?

16. What is the difference between a summary sheet and a standard Cornell-style note sheet?

17. What advantage do advanced summary sheets provide over regular summary sheets?

18. In what situations should you cram?

19. How do you cram systematically?

20. What is the word to remember if you find you are forced to cram?

21. What role should your notes and your textbooks play in cramming?

22. How does it help to recite your material both out loud and on paper as a test draws nearer?

Preparing Yourself Mentally

23. How does mental preparation help eliminate test anxiety?

24. What can you ask the instructor directly about an exam?

25. Why is it helpful to look over past exams?

26. What advantage can you gain by becoming familiar with the testing site?

27. What should you do if you cannot study at the actual test site?

28. How does your attitude affect your mental preparation?

29. What can you do to relax in preparation for an exam?

30. How can you use self-talk constructively?

31. How can visualization affect your chances of success?

CHAPTER 15 MASTERING OBJECTIVE TESTS

1. What does mastering an objective test involve?

Understanding the Kinds of Objective Questions

2. What is the basic idea behind answering a true-false question?

3. What makes marking a true-false statement difficult?

4. What is the format for a typical multiple-choice question?

5. In what three ways can multiple-choice questions be more difficult than true-false statements?

6. How do you determine the relationship between a matching question's two columns?
7. What are the pitfalls of matching carelessly or guessing prematurely?
8. What is the makeup of a typical sentence-completion question?
9. How are sentence-completion questions like multiple-choice questions?

Choosing Effective Study Methods

10. What is the safest way of preparing for an objective test?
11. What is the advantage of learning information to the point of recall?
12. What are the advantages of the Questions-in-the-Margin System?
13. What advantage is there in being a study "switch hitter"?

Moving Systematically Through the Test

14. How do you move systematically through a test?
15. How do qualifiers affect the meaning of an objective question?
16. What are 100 percent words, and how do they affect the meaning of an objective question?
17. How should you cope with qualifiers?
18. What is the Goldilocks Technique?
19. What is the greatest danger of negatives?
20. How do grammatical rules help you determine answers for objective questions?
21. How can you determine whether an answer is the best response or simply a good one?
22. How should you handle questions you're unsure of?

Learning Strategies for Specific Question Types

23. Which response should you mark if you're stumped by a true-false statement?
24. Why should longer true-false statements be viewed with suspicion?
25. How can you confirm that "all of the above" is the correct option?
26. What is the true-false technique, and why is it helpful?
27. How do you effectively answer matching questions?

28. What is the best method for handling an ambiguous sentence-completion question?

29. How should the length of the blank affect your choice in a sentence-completion question?

30. How should you handle a sentence-completion question that contains two blanks that are widely separated?

CHAPTER 16 TACKLING ESSAY TESTS

1. How do the demands of an essay test differ from those of an objective test?

2. How do you write thoughtful, forceful essays?

Moving Through the Test Systematically

3. How can you move through an essay test systematically?

4. How should you address any ideas that occur to you just as the exam is about to begin?

5. Why are essay directions so important?

6. Why should you read all the questions in advance?

7. How should you manage your time when taking an essay exam?

8. What should you do if you're running out of time?

9. What should you do if you finish the essay test early?

10. Why should you answer the easiest question first?

Learning the Basics of Writing an Essay Exam

11. What role does precision play in understanding and answering an essay question?

12. What skills are required to provide the correct essay answer?

13. How does knowing your instructor's pet ideas affect your answers?

Writing Effectively Under Time Constraints

14. How can you ensure that your essay gets right to the point?

15. What is the danger of beginning your essay with an introduction?

16. What should your essay's opening sentence contain?

17. Would you be "jumping the gun" if you put your answer in the first sentence of the essay?

18. What are the dangers of wordy writing?

19. How can you make your answer both clear and obvious?

20. What is the most straightforward way of organizing your essay?

21. How can the question serve as a clue for the way you should organize your essay answer?

22. How are transitions helpful in an essay answer?

23. How should you end your essay?

24. How can you make your essay look neater?

25. What is the advantage of leaving extra space around your essays?

Supporting Your Points

26. How can you ensure that your essay is well supported?

27. What is the purpose of most of the sentences in your essay?

28. Do generally accepted opinions require supporting evidence?

29. Are personal opinions appropriate in an essay answer?

CHAPTER 17   STUDYING MATHEMATICS

How to Remedy a Weak Background

1. In what ways is doing mathematics like solving puzzles? In what ways is it much more complex?

2. Explain how a hole in someone's early mathematics background can affect that person's understanding of college mathematics.

3. List some nonmathematics courses you've taken in which mathematics had an important role. What areas of mathematics were used in each of these courses?

How to Develop Good Study Habits

4. Why is it so crucial that you keep up to date in a math course?
5. If you take minimal notes in class, can you still read your textbook for full understanding? Why or why not?
6. Describe the methods cited for using your textbook in a math course.
7. Why would you need to review for mathematics tests if you keep up your daily work?

Practical Suggestions for Problem Solving

8. Describe the first step involved in solving a math problem.
9. How is calculating different from analyzing? When should you begin to calculate in solving a math problem?
10. How can drawing a diagram be of help to you?
11. List the advantages cited to using your calculator.

How to Attack a Nonroutine Problem

12. Explain the strategies for solving routine and nonroutine problems. How are they different?
13. What is the immediate goal of the problem-solving strategies presented?

CHAPTER 18   LEARNING WITH THE COMPUTER

1. What does the term *computer literate* mean? What defines someone who is computer literate?

Debunking Myths About Computers

2. Six myths about learning with the computer are discussed in this chapter. What are these myths? List some of the ways in which you can overcome any initial misgivings you may have about computers.
3. How do computer programming courses and those that teach the basic applications (word processing, spreadsheet accounting, and database management) differ from one another?

Identifying Your School's Computer Resources

4. What are the general steps advised for identifying your school's computer resources?

5. How can advance work with your textbook help you prepare for a computer course? How is this preparation similar to that of other courses? What would you imagine to be the major difference?

6. How should you learn about the computer lab facilities at your school?

7. Define these computer terms:
   a. word processing
   b. software
   c. terminal
   d. mainframe
   e. microcomputer
   f. printer
   g. letter-quality printer
   h. dot matrix printer
   i. hard copy
   j. password
   k. file
   l. spreadsheet accounting
   m. database management program
   n. floppy disk

Determining Your Computer Needs

8. What steps can you take to determine your computer requirements?

Applications

9. Describe how a word-processing program works. What are some of the ways in which a word processor can help you with writing a paper?

10. Describe how the following features of many word-processing programs work:
    a. spelling checker
    b. electronic thesaurus
    c. style checker

11. How can word-processing programs help you plan a study schedule or calendar?

12. Describe how a spreadsheet accounting program works. What are some of the uses to which such a program can be put?
13. Describe the "filing system" analogy and how it relates to a database management program.
14. How is concept mapping similar to the database management program?

Using the Computer in the Library

15. How can using the computer in the library increase your efficiency with research?
16. Describe how an in-library bibliographic search works.
17. How are off-campus bibliographic searches different from in-library searches?

Computer-Aided Learning

18. What does the term *computer-aided learning* mean?
19. Describe tutorial software. What course(s) could a tutorial program assist you in?
20. What distinguishes tutorial software from other types of computer-aided learning?
21. What does simulation software do? In what kinds of courses is it most applicable?
22. What are the benefits of educational games?

Continuing to Learn

23. What are some of the ways in which you can continue to learn with the computer?

3

Part Three

SUPPLEMENTARY CHAPTERS

A   Writing a Research Paper
B   Studying Science
C   Studying Foreign Languages
D   Studying Literature

If your writing falls apart, it probably has no primary ideas to hold it together

SHERIDAN BAKER

Professor, author of The Practical Stylist

A

Supplementary Chapter A

WRITING A RESEARCH PAPER

From the time it is assigned until the day it is due, a research paper can occupy your mind like no other type of assignment. Although writing a research paper can be time consuming, it doesn't have to be overwhelming if you take the process one step at a time. To give you a head start in the art of the research paper, this chapter provides a calm and well-organized system for

- Deciding what to investigate
- Gathering information
- Devising a framework
- Writing the paper

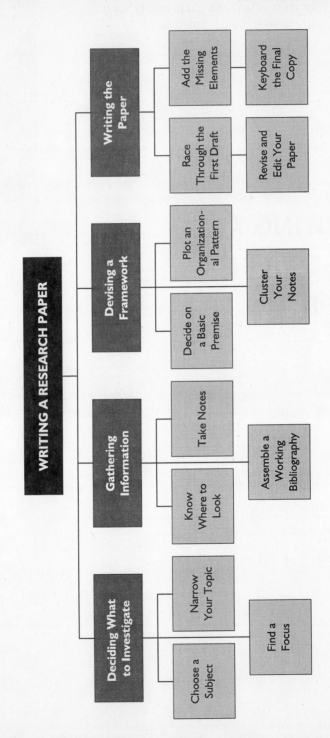

WRITING A RESEARCH PAPER

Deciding What to Investigate
- Choose a Subject
- Narrow Your Topic
- Find a Focus

Gathering Information
- Know Where to Look
- Take Notes
- Assemble a Working Bibliography

Devising a Framework
- Decide on a Basic Premise
- Plot an Organizational Pattern
- Cluster Your Notes

Writing the Paper
- Race Through the First Draft
- Add the Missing Elements
- Revise and Edit Your Paper
- Keyboard the Final Copy

Writing even a modest research paper can take a lot of effort. Yet though the task is long, the skills it requires aren't sophisticated, and most of them aren't new. In fact, writing a paper isn't much more difficult than reading about a subject in detail, taking notes on your reading, organizing your notes, and reciting—all the activities you undertake to prepare for a test or quiz. The difference is that instead of reciting out loud, you put your recitation on paper in a form that makes what you've learned readable for others. If you realize that writing a paper is not much different from studying your notes, and if you systematically decide what to write about, gather information, devise a framework, and then do the actual writing, you may even find that writing papers can be a most absorbing way to learn about a subject.

DECIDING WHAT TO INVESTIGATE

Finding a suitable topic is often the biggest stumbling block in research. It's essential that you know how to choose a topic easily and efficiently. There are three steps in the process of selecting a topic: Begin with a general subject that interests you, narrow it down, and then sharpen it even further by finding a focus. If you follow these steps, you'll wind up with a topic that is both interesting and specific.

Choose a Subject

In most cases, you'll be selecting a topic from a broad subject area. Because you'll be spending a great deal of time on the subject, your best bet is to choose one you are interested in or can develop an interest in. And if it isn't a subject that others are researching, then so much the better.

If you aren't sure what subject to select, do some preliminary research at the library. Scanning the bookshelves in your area of interest, consulting the *Reader's Guide to Periodical Literature* or a computerized periodical listing, and asking for assistance from a reference librarian will introduce you to an array of possible topics. In addition, the trip to the library will warm you up for the full-fledged research that lies ahead.

Suppose you are fascinated by natural disasters and want to learn more about them. But the subject "natural disasters" includes scores of topics: droughts, floods, tornadoes, hurricanes, volcanoes, and earthquakes, to name just a few. How can you do justice to them all? Obviously, you can't. You must narrow your topic.

Narrow Your Topic

Selecting a topic that interests you is just the beginning. The most common criticism of a research paper is that its topic is too broad. A Cornell professor of English suggests this method for narrowing your topic: Put your subject through three or four significant narrowings, moving from a given category to a class within that category each time. This method is similar to the Silver Dollar System (see Chapter 5), which enables you to select the main ideas from your notes.

For example, if you select natural disasters as the topic for a ten-to-fifteen page research paper, you have to narrow the scope of your topic before you can cover it in adequate depth. Three narrowings will probably reduce the subject down to a manageable size, although four may be necessary.

General Topic: Natural Disasters

First narrowing: earthquakes

Second narrowing: earthquake prediction

Third narrowing: scientific developments in earthquake prediction

Fourth narrowing: computer simulations in earthquake prediction

Concept maps, which are explained in Chapter 13 and are similar to those in this book, can be used to "visually" narrow a topic. Write your general subject on a blank sheet of paper and circle it. Next write down subtopics of your general subject, circle each, and connect them with lines to the general subject. Then write and circle subtopics of your subtopics. At this point, you may have a suitably narrow subject. If not, keep adding levels of subtopics until you arrive at one. (See Figure A.1.) The advantage of narrowing your topic with a concept map is that you provide yourself with a number of alternate topics should your original topic choice prove unworkable.

Find a Focus

Once you've narrowed your topic, give your research direction and purpose by developing a compelling question about your topic. The information you gather from your research can then be used to develop an answer. For the topic "The use of computer simulations in earthquake prediction," you might ask, "How helpful are computer simulations in earthquake prediction?"

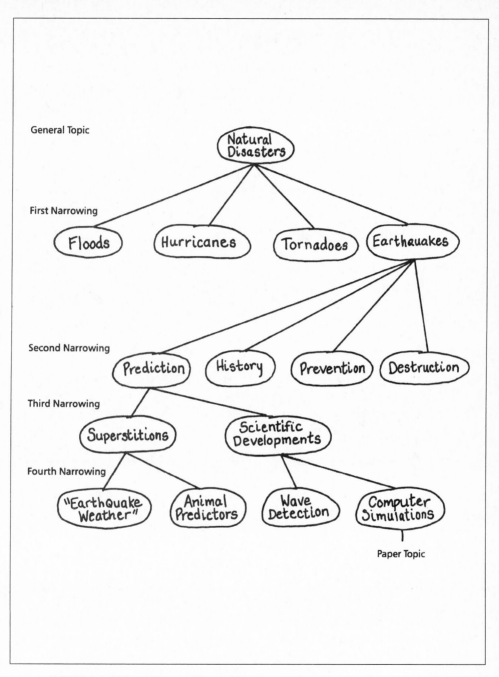

General Topic

Natural Disasters

First Narrowing

Floods   Hurricanes   Tornadoes   Earthquakes

Second Narrowing

Prediction   History   Prevention   Destruction

Third Narrowing

Superstitions   Scientific Developments

Fourth Narrowing

"Earthquake Weather"   Animal Predictors   Wave Detection   Computer Simulations

Paper Topic

FIGURE A.1   Using a Concept Map to Narrow a Topic

Whether you actually arrive at a definitive answer to your research question isn't crucial. The important thing is to focus your research efforts on answering the broad question.

GATHERING INFORMATION

The next step in your research is to begin gathering information. That requires knowing where to look (and knowing what you're looking for), building a working bibliography, and then taking detailed notes.

Know Where to Look

Unless you're using firsthand information—from interviews or experiments—nearly all your material will come from the library. During this stage of your investigation, the library's most valuable resources will be the reference librarian, indexes, periodicals, and books.

Get Help from the Reference Librarian　Before you begin your research, as well as any time during the process when you hit a snag, seek out the reference librarian. Although librarians may not be experts on your particular subject, they *are* experts at using the library's research tools. Librarians can often suggest indexes you may not have heard of, sources you didn't think to consult, and searching strategies you didn't try.

Consult Periodical Indexes　Most of your research will come from periodicals and books. It's wise to consult the articles that relate to your paper topic before you begin to delve into books. Not only do periodicals frequently provide the most recent information on a subject; sometimes they supply the only information. In addition, articles often include important names and titles that relate to your subject and occasionally provide a valuable overview of your topic.

There are a number of general and specific indexes, both bound and computerized, for periodicals.

Use Bound Indexes.　The most prevalent bound index is the *Reader's Guide to Periodical Literature*. Each volume lists by author and subject all the articles that appeared in several dozen magazines during a given year. To locate articles on your topic, consult the years in which you think those articles may have been published. Each entry in the *Reader's Guide* gives you the information you need to locate the appropriate journal or magazine.

Your paper topic may pertain to a subject that has its own index. For example, if you are doing research in psychology, you can refer to several indexes that deal specifically with psychology and that include journals and magazines that aren't listed in the *Reader's Guide*. A number of other subjects, such as business and education, have their own indexes. In addition, large newspapers such as the *New York Times* publish indexes of their articles.

Use Computerized Indexes.   Many libraries now use computerized magazine indexes such as Info-trac that enable you to type in the name of a subject, author, or title and receive a list of relevant articles. You may also be able to customize your search with key words and/or Boolean searching.

Key word search. Key words can provide the most direct route to the articles you are seeking, especially when searching by subject isn't convenient or fruitful. For example, if you want information about Gregg Toland, the cinematographer who worked with Orson Welles on the movie *Citizen Kane*, you may come up empty if you use the subjects "Toland" or "Citizen Kane" in your search. The database simply may not have enough articles on these topics to justify a separate subject heading. If, however, you search for articles under a broader subject, such as "Motion pictures—American," you may have to scan through hundreds of citations before you find appropriate ones. With a key word search, by contrast, you can type in a word (or name) such as "Toland," and the computer will reply with every article in its database that contains the key word you have typed.

Boolean search. A Boolean search enables you to narrow your search by combining two key words. Suppose you need information about the Detroit Lions football team. If you searched under the subject "Detroit," "Football," or "Lions," you would have to scan thousands of citations that have nothing to do with your particular topic. But by searching for titles that contain both key words—"Football" and "Lions"—you are likelier to pinpoint articles that deal directly with your topic.

These computerized indexes have some advantages over bound indexes and some disadvantages as well.

Advantages

Speed.   If you know what you're looking for, you can usually come up with a list of periodical entries in less than a minute.

Consolidation.   Unlike many bound indexes, which have a separate volume for each year, a computerized index normally includes a wide range of years. A single computerized search can cover more ground.

A written record.   Most computerized indexes are connected to a printer. Once you find the sources you are looking for, you can print out the citations immediately.

Abstracts.   Some computerized citations include an abstract that summarizes the points of the articles and that helps you determine whether it would be worth your while to read.

Disadvantages

Limited listings.   Most computer indexes list only relatively recent entries. If you're searching for an article that is more than fifteen years old, for example, you will probably have to look for the citation in a bound index.

Outdated information.   The information in a computerized index is stored on a compact disc, which must be replaced whenever the listings need to be updated. Some libraries update their discs frequently; others do not.

Limited availability.   If the wait at the computer index looks long, you may be wise to do your research with the bound indexes instead. The time-saving advantage of the computer index will be lost if you have to wait too long to use it.

Consult Book Indexes   Books usually have their own indexes—on individual cards or in a computer.

Use a Card Catalog.   The card catalog generally consists of several large cabinets and a series of long, small drawers divided by author, title, and subject and arranged alphabetically. To use the card catalog effectively, you may need to use the author, the title, and the subject sections. If you know the names of experts in the area you are researching or if you're already aware of titles of books on the subject, you'll want to consult both the author and title catalogs. If while scanning articles in magazines or journals you've uncovered the names of authors or books that relate to your subject, you'll want to find out whether your library has any of these books. Finally, you'll want to check in the subject catalog for other books pertaining to your topic.

Use a Computerized Catalog.   Many libraries have replaced the traditional card catalog with a set of computer terminals that enable you to quickly find the same information without flipping through dozens of index cards. Instead of scanning a large list of books, as you did with the card catalog, you simply type in the information you are seeking and the computer responds. Like the traditional card catalog, most computer catalogs allow you to search for a book based on its subject, title, or author. In addition, many computer catalogs include advanced commands similar to those used with the periodical index.

Assemble a Working Bibliography

As you discover magazines and books that relate to your research, add them to a *working bibliography*—a list of promising sources that you plan to consult. Be generous in compiling your list. It's better to check out several references that do not help than to miss a good one because its title isn't appealing.

Instead of listing all these references on a large sheet of paper, you can use a separate 3 × 5 card for each reference. Then later on, if you decide that a particular reference doesn't help, you can simply throw away its card.

Figure A.2 provides an efficient format for putting your bibliography on 3 × 5 cards. On the front of the card, record the following information:

The name of the library where the periodical or book is located

A short title of your subject. A title will make it easier to locate a particular card and will aid in clustering your information.

The library call number

The reference information—that is, the author, title, publishing data, and page references—in exactly the form that you plan to use it in the bibliographical portion of your paper. This ensures that you will include all the essential parts of the reference and that typing your paper will be much easier.

On the back of the card, jot down your assessment of the reference. If the source doesn't seem useful, then briefly explain why. If the source appears helpful, jot down how. Then when you have a chance to take another look at the article or book, you'll know why you thought it would or would not be useful. And if you shift the focus of your paper, you'll be able to determine whether sources you had eliminated should now be consulted and whether previously promising sources will no longer be of help.

Olin Library	Theories of Memory
Q 360 .C33	Campbell, Jeremy Grammatical Man. New York: Simon & Schuster, Inc., 1982.

3 x 5 Card with Data

Bottom-up and top-down theories of memory described in Chapter 18.

Refers back to previous chapters and is difficult to read in spots. Provides solid summary of the two theories.
Uses simple, vivid examples to explain difficult points.

Reverse of 3 x 5 Card with Comments

FIGURE A.2 Working Bibliography: 3 × 5 Card Method

Take Notes

Using your bibliography as a springboard, you can investigate your sources and begin taking notes. There's no getting around it—taking notes is time consuming. But if your notes are easy to use, neat, brief, and accurate, then the bulk of your paper will be written by the time you have completed the note-taking step.

Making Sure Your Notes Are Easy to Use To make your notes easy to use, jot each note on a separate piece of paper rather than writing them one after the other on regular-sized sheets. Three-by-five-inch index cards are commonly used for notes, although you can use slips of paper instead. Whether you use cards or slips, you will be able to rearrange them easily and often because each note is separate.

Another way to make your notes easier to use is by conscientiously identifying each card or slip. In the top left corner, write the author's name or the title of the source you consulted. Then at the bottom right, jot down the specific page on which you found the information. With these two markings on every note card, you can easily verify or add to any information you've gathered for your paper. In addition, you'll have all the information you may need for your citations (see Figure A.3).

Keep Your Note Cards Neat Detailed notes are useless if you can't read them. Write your notes neatly the first time, even if it takes a little longer to do so. Use the modified printing system (see Chapter 10) to write quickly but legibly, and write in pen, instead of pencil, to avoid smears and fading.

Keep Your Note Cards Brief Brevity is the secret behind a useful note card. Get to the heart of the matter with each note you take. Make your notes concise, yet sufficiently detailed to provide accurate meaning.

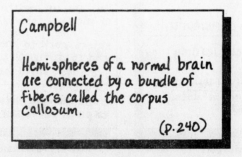

FIGURE A.3   Detailed Note Written on One Side of a 3 × 5 Card

One simple way to limit the length of each note card is by abbreviating common words. For example, use *w/* instead of "with," *co.* instead of "company," and *govt* in place of "government." Develop your own abbreviations for words you commonly use. For example, if you're doing research on earthquakes, you may want to use *RS* to stand for "Richter scale" and *tct plates* to abbreviate "tectonic plates." Be careful not to go overboard with abbreviations, however. Abbreviating words may save you time to begin with, but you don't want to waste that time later trying to decipher your unfamiliar shorthand.

Strive for Accuracy   Because you're dealing in facts, you must make certain that the information you jot down is accurate. It's relatively easy to remember as you're taking notes who said what and which of the thoughts you are writing down are your own and which are the thoughts of the author. But between the time you fill your last note card and the moment you write the first line of your paper, you're liable to forget these crucial details. To counteract forgetting and to ensure the information in your paper is accurate, distinguish clearly on your note cards between quoted ideas and paraphrased ideas and between the writer's thoughts and your own.

Copy Quotations Carefully.   When you quote from a book or an article, make sure that you do so carefully. Place quotation marks on your card around the exact words you copied from the reference. Compare your version with the original quotation to make sure you copied it correctly. Don't change the wording or the spelling of the author's quotation. If you find a misspelling or a grammatical error in the quotation, you may use the bracketed notation [sic] to make it clear to your reader that you're aware of the mistake.

If you leave out a section or even one word from a quote, use three ellipsis points (. . .) to indicate the omission. If the words you left out came at the end of a sentence, add a period before the ellipses.

The purpose of an ellipsis is to leave out information that doesn't relate to the point you are using the quotation to support. An ellipsis should not be used to rearrange a quotation simply to suit your needs. Ellipses are intended to abbreviate a quotation, not alter its meaning.

Mark Thoughts of Your Own.   Some of your best ideas may occur as you're taking notes. Put these thoughts on paper right away, but do so on a separate note card marked "my idea" or something similar. That way you'll be sure not to confuse your original ideas with the ones you've encountered in your reading.

Paraphrase What You Read.   Although it is important to distinguish your original ideas from the ones you have read, there's nothing wrong with paraphrasing—expressing someone else's ideas in your own words—as long as you give proper credit to the source. If you paraphrase as you take notes, you'll often be able to transfer what you've written on your note cards to your draft without changing a word.

DEVISING A FRAMEWORK

You can devise a solid framework for your paper out of a pile of disconnected note cards by deciding on a basic premise, clustering your notes under a handful of main ideas, and plotting out a clear, logical organizational pattern.

Decide on a Basic Premise

In the same way that choosing a focus helped provide direction for your research, deciding on a basic *premise* from the notes you now have lays the foundation for your paper's organization. Potential arguments, apparent similarities, and possible theories all have a way of rising to the surface in the process of taking notes. Any of these can be used to form a basic premise, which is the fundamental approach that underlies your paper. If a premise doesn't become obvious to you as you're taking notes, go back over the information and ask yourself some hard questions. For example:

Where is this paper heading?

What are the ramifications of the information I've assembled?

What point is most important?

What am I saying?

What do I want to say?

If there's a choice of viewpoint—for or against a question, for example— which view has the most evidence to support it? If you've done a good job of research, you should be able to decide now what you want to say in your paper, and you should have the evidence to support that view right on your 3 × 5 cards.

Cluster Your Notes

The paper's basic premise should act as a magnet for clustering your notes, which enables you to draw out the most important ideas from the dozens and perhaps hundreds of notes you have written. In most cases, a research paper should incorporate fewer than seven main ideas. These ideas will form the framework for your paper. The cards that remain won't be wasted but will be used as support for the more important ideas. Of course, if a note isn't important enough to be considered a main idea and doesn't provide support for the main ideas, that note should be left out of your paper.

Choosing the main ideas and clustering your research notes require selectivity, the same skill you used not only in narrowing your original paper topic but in studying conventional notes as well (see Chapter 5). In fact, if you find it difficult to pick out a handful of main ideas from a pile of notes, apply the following three-step system to help pinpoint the pillars that will form your paper's supports.

1. Read through your note cards and pick out those cards that seem more important than the others.
2. Now that you have two piles of notes instead of one, pick up the smaller pile and repeat the process, pulling out the most important notes and using them to make up a third pile.
3. Finally, pick up the third pile, which by now should contain only a dozen or so note cards, and find four or five ideas that seem to be the most important ones. These ideas will be the basis of your premise and of the pattern for your paper.

Plot an Organizational Pattern

Your basic premise and personal choice largely determine the pattern your paper will follow. You could use any of the organizational patterns listed in Chapter 8 as the framework for your paper. The time pattern or the process pattern is appropriate for most college papers. For some papers, however, you may be required to develop an argument. A good pattern for such papers is to begin with a statement of your premise and then support it with logical examples that build to a conclusion. This kind of organization affords more flexibility than the others.

You may need to experiment with several patterns before you arrive at a framework that adequately accommodates the information you want to include in your paper. Don't be discouraged by the inevitable period of trial and error.

There's no one "correct" way of plotting your paper. You may feel most comfortable using a traditional outline. Or you may find the process of *mapping* easier and more enjoyable.

To map out your research paper, use the index cards that contain your paper's main ideas and subideas (or jot these ideas down on small slips of paper). On a clear surface such as a desk or a tabletop, shift the cards around like checkers on a checkerboard, clustering them in various ways, according to the premise of your paper.

If you're planning to structure your paper using the time or process pattern, arrange your ideas so they follow logically from the earliest to the latest or from the start of the process to the end. If you're structuring your paper as an argument, decide which of the major points should be made first; then arrange the remaining points in an order that will make your argument smooth, logical, and easy to follow.

The chapter maps in this book provide examples of the process and argument patterns. The map in this chapter, for example, uses the process pattern, spelling out in order, the steps for writing a research paper. The map for the text's Chapter 14, in contrast, develops an argument; it asserts a premise—managing test anxiety requires preparation—and supports the premise by detailing the ways to prepare.

When you arrive at an arrangement that incorporates your information and makes logical sense, you have found a suitable pattern for your paper. Once you have arranged the cards that contain your major points in an effective order, repeat the procedure by arranging the cards that contain your minor points. Think of each major point as a premise in itself. Then arrange the minor points that support a major point in a clear and effective way.

If, as you arrange your cards, you find gaps in your organization, you may need to create new categories or perhaps even return to the library to take more notes.

Finally, with all points arranged to your satisfaction, go back and number your cards according to the order in which they'll appear in your paper.

WRITING THE PAPER

You already have most of your paper worked out—information, sources, organization. Now all you have to do is put your data into sentences and paragraphs and work up a first draft of your paper. Once that is accomplished, allow yourself plenty of time to go back and revise and edit what you've written, add the missing elements, and type or keyboard the final copy.

Race Through the First Draft

The best way to start writing is simply to write. Pausing with your pen poised over an empty page or with your fingers resting idly on a keyboard waiting for inspiration to strike is a useless endeavor. Inspiration, like concentration, seldom comes when you call it. Once your hands are engaged in the physical motions of writing, your brain will follow.

Write your first draft as rapidly and spontaneously as possible. To ensure continuity, record your thoughts on paper as they go through your mind. Don't stop to ponder alternatives. Although you will probably write too much, don't be concerned; it's easier to cut out than to add.

In your first draft your goal is simply to transfer information from your notes to your paper. Take each card in order and write. Start with major point one. State what it is, and then use supporting evidence to show why it is so. As you use a reference from the card, note the card number on your paper. You can put the footnotes in later, taking the exact information from the card. Continue to write, following your organized and numbered cards.

Only after you've completed your first draft should you step back and take a look at what you've written. If you typed your draft into a computer, print out a hard copy so you can jot down your comments. Regardless of whether your draft was handwritten, typewritten, or printed by a computer, go over what you've written and pencil in changes, adding words or phrases and circling lines or paragraphs you want to move or remove. Figure A.4 shows a page from a first draft, complete with annotations, insertions, and other marginal markings.

While your markings are still fresh in your mind, write or type a clear copy that incorporates all your changes. Don't wait before adding in these corrections. If you delay even a day, you may lose a lot of time trying to recall exactly what you meant by some of your notes. And if you type or rewrite the material while it's still fresh, you may find that you do some spontaneous revision.

Once you have made these changes, put your draft aside for a while. To gain objectivity about what is in the paper and what is still missing, you need a cooling off period of at least a day. When you return to your paper, you'll then easily spot errors and weaknesses in your writing.

Revise and Edit Your Paper

The hardest part of writing a research paper is completing the first draft. From that point on, you'll be refining what you've already written. In the next drafts—and you may write two, three, or even four drafts before you are satisfied with your paper—you'll focus on strengthening supporting evidence and fine-tuning technical details such as transitions, grammar, and spelling.

Strengthen Supporting Evidence Students often state a main point and then go on to something else without supporting it. The kinds of evidence you need to support a major point are statistics, quotations from other published

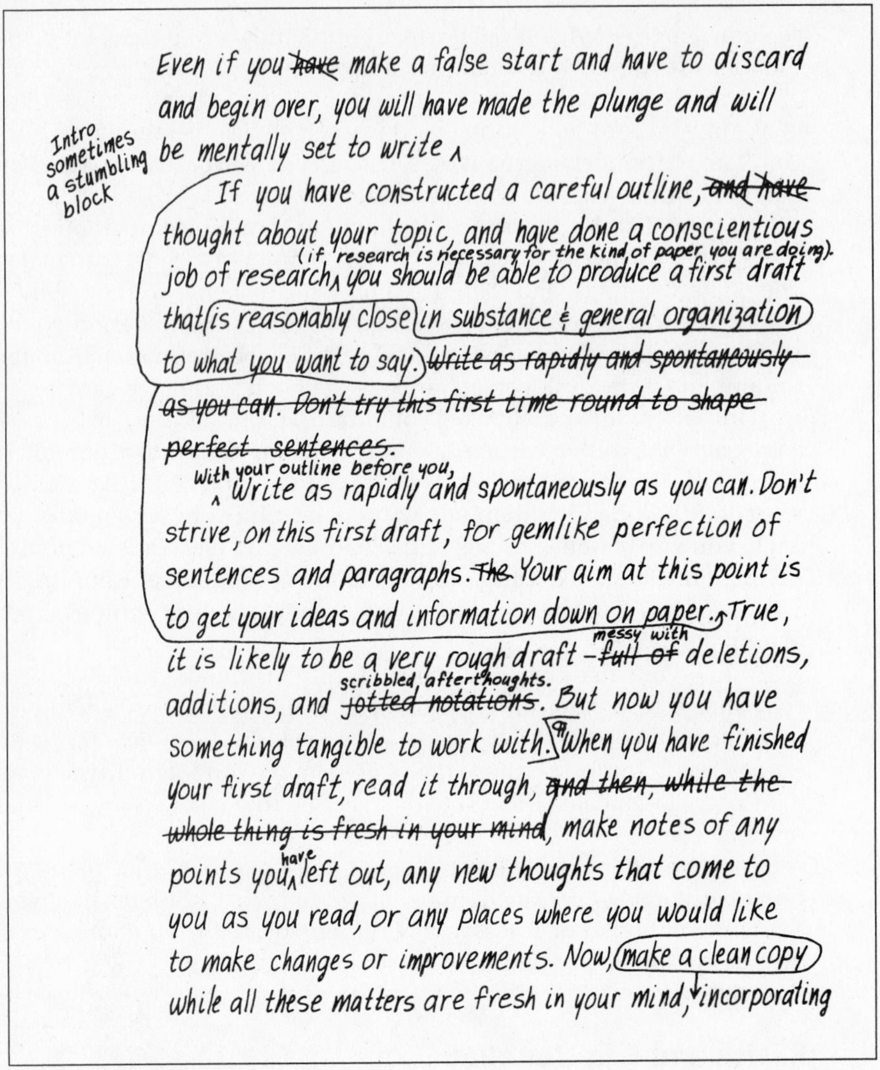

Even if you ~~have~~ make a false start and have to discard and begin over, you will have made the plunge and will be mentally set to write ‸

Intro sometimes a stumbling block

    If you have constructed a careful outline, ~~and have~~ thought about your topic, and have done a conscientious job of research‸ *(if research is necessary for the kind of paper you are doing).* you should be able to produce a first draft that ⟨is reasonably close⟩ in substance & general organization to what you want to say. ~~Write as rapidly and spontaneously as you can. Don't try this first time round to shape perfect sentences.~~

With your outline before you,
‸ Write as rapidly and spontaneously as you can. Don't strive, on this first draft, for gemlike perfection of sentences and paragraphs. ~~The~~ Your aim at this point is to get your ideas and information down on paper. ‸True, it is likely to be a very rough draft ~~full of~~ *messy with* deletions, additions, and ~~jotted notations~~ *scribbled afterthoughts*. But now you have something tangible to work with. ¶When you have finished your first draft, read it through, ~~and then, while the whole thing is fresh in your mind~~, make notes of any points you‸ *have* left out, any new thoughts that come to you as you read, or any places where you would like to make changes or improvements. Now, ⟨make a clean copy⟩ while all these matters are fresh in your mind, ‸incorporating

FIGURE A.4 Page from a First Draft

works, facts, examples, comparisons and contrasts in views, expert opinion, and description. If you make statements and follow them up with generalities, you will not convince your reader that your main point is true. Use what you have collected on your cards to support your points. Here, with examples, are the steps you can take to develop a major point:

1. State your point clearly.

   The two sides of the human brain perform distinct functions.

2. Develop the point beyond a brief statement.

   According to the theory of brain laterality, the left hemisphere of the brain handles analytical thinking, while the right hemisphere is the home of abstract thought.

3. Support with data from authorities and with statistics.

   Drs. Michael Gazzaniga and Roger Sperry found that the cerebral hemispheres process information differently (add reference here). Subsequent research determined that the brain's left and right sides contrast information that is symbolic and conceptual versus information that is nonsymbolic and directly perceived.

4. Illustrate with examples.

   For example, if you were to add up a column of numbers, you would probably be using the left side of your brain. But if you were sketching a picture, you would be engaging the right side.

Be sure that all the main points are supported equally with this kind of evidence. If you can't find enough evidence to support one point, perhaps it's not a major one. You may need to reorganize the structure to include that point under one of the other major points.

Avoid padding. You may be tempted to add words or to rephrase a point to make the paper longer. Such padding is obvious to the reader, who's looking for logical arguments and good sense, and will not improve your grade. If you haven't enough evidence to support a statement, leave it out or get more information.

Fine-Tune Technical Details Although awkward transitions, clumsy grammar, and poor spelling may not affect the basic meaning of your paper, they do affect the reader's perception of how you have thought about your topic and what you have written.

Provide Transitions. In writing your paper, consider how to help your readers move easily from one main point to the next. If they feel that there's no connection, they will find it hard to follow the logical sequence that you have established in your own mind. You must therefore use transitional words and phrases to make your paper easy to follow. (See Chapter 8 for a list of these words.) Check carefully for transitions, and insert them where they are needed.

Correct Grammar. Students who use the English language correctly get their ideas across to other people more clearly and forcibly than do those who stumble over every sentence. Moreover, students who apply the rules of grammar in their papers earn better grades. If you are unsure about these rules or careless with them, your meaning may get lost. If you feel that you could use a review of grammar, there are good texts that give you the elements of English grammar by a programmed method. Some of them are even fun to read.

Here's a brief list of some popular handbooks of English grammar:

Corder, Jim W. *Handbook of Current English,* 8th ed. Glenview, Ill.: Scott, Foresman, 1989.

Diamond, Harriet, and Phyllis Dutwin. *Grammar in Plain English,* 3rd ed. New York: Barron's Educational Series, 1997.

Feigenbaum, Irwin. *The Grammar Handbook.* New York: Oxford University Press, 1987.

Hodges, John C. et al. *Harbrace College Handbook,* 13th ed. San Diego, Calif.: Harcourt Brace Jovanovich, 1998.

Shertzer, Margaret D. *The Elements of Grammar.* Macmillan Publishing, 1996.

Check Spelling. If your spelling problems are not severe, you will find a dictionary helpful. If your spelling is poor, look for one of the paperback books that list the most commonly misspelled words. If you cannot recognize that you are spelling words incorrectly, have someone who is good at spelling read your paper and mark, not correct, the words that are wrong. Then look up and insert the correct spellings. If you do this conscientiously over a period of time, you will improve your spelling.

Of course, if you are writing your paper on a computer, you can use a spell-checking program to pinpoint your spelling mistakes. The spell-checker compares each word you have typed with the words stored in its dictionary and calls your attention to words that don't appear there. Although the computer can catch many of your spelling errors, it isn't infallible. The size of the dictionary is limited, and the spell-checker is unable to recognize words that are spelled correctly but used incorrectly (such as *there* instead of *their*).

Add the Missing Elements

Having revised and edited your writing, you can now add the missing elements that will make your paper complete. Because your paper is a research paper, you must give credit for your information by including citations and a bibliography. In addition, the paper will need a title, an introduction, and a conclusion.

Give Credit Where It's Needed To avoid any appearance of plagiarism and to demonstrate the depth of your research, attribute quoted or paraphrased material and include a bibliography.

Avoid Plagiarism. Plagiarism is stealing other people's words and ideas and making them appear to be your own. It need not be as blatant as copying whole passages without giving credit. If you paraphrase something from already published material and do not cite your source, you're guilty of plagiarism even though you may have no intention of stealing. Simply rearranging sentences or rephrasing a little without crediting is still plagiarism.

Those who grade papers are quick to notice a change in writing style from one of your papers to another or from one part of your paper to another. Your writing is like your fingerprints—individual. If you try to use another's work, his or her style will not match the rest of your paper, and the difference will be obvious. Instructors may give you the benefit of the doubt if they cannot prove where you got plagiarized material. But if they can—and doing so is usually not difficult—plagiarism is grounds for expulsion from college. In a world where the written word is a major product, stealing it from someone else is a serious offense.

Include Citations. Avoid plagiarism by crediting material you've quoted or paraphrased to its source. You may include a credit right after the quoted material, within the body of the paper, in a format like this: (Jones 1996, p. 264). This citation refers to page 264 of the work by Jones that was published in 1996 and is listed in your bibliography. Or you can use a superscript [1] and cite the full source at the bottom of the page or in a complete listing at the end of the paper. Credits that appear at the bottom of the page are called *footnotes.* Figure A.5 shows a format for footnotes and for credits at the end of the paper. References are numbered in the order in which they appear in your paper. Other forms are given in handbooks on English usage.

Supply a Bibliography. The bibliography lists the sources you cite in your credits and may include other books or published material that you read as

---

1. Richard Webster, *Why Freud Was Wrong* (New York: Basic Books, 1995), pp. 136–154.
2. Glenn Alan Cheney, *Journey to Chernobyl* (Chicago, Ill.: Academy Chicago Publishers), p. 107.

FIGURE A.5   Format for Footnotes and End-of-Paper Credits

background for the paper but did not quote. A bibliography is not "notes," "endnotes," or "sources." It is a listing of the books that you used in preparing the paper, and you should use the correct title for this listing. When you compile the bibliography, use the 3 × 5 cards you prepared earlier. Each entry should include enough information so that a reader can identify the work and find it in a library.

Entries are listed alphabetically by author. Different bibliographic forms are used in different fields. Either select a standard form from a handbook on English usage, or follow the form used in one of the journals on your subject.

Ask your reference librarian to assist you in finding the style manual for a specific field such as biology, chemistry, law, mathematics, physics, psychology, and so forth.

The following three widely used general style manuals will provide you with a form for your citations and bibliography:

Gibaldi, Joseph. *The MLA Style Manual.* New York: The Modern Language Association of America, 1999.

The Chicago Manual of Style. 14th ed. Chicago: University of Chicago Press, 1993.

Merriam-Webster's Standard American Style Manual. Springfield, Mass.: Merriam-Webster, 1993.

No matter what form you use, follow it consistently for every entry in your bibliography. Figure A.6 shows a common bibliographic form.

Choose a Suitable Title   It is often a good idea to wait until you have written the paper before you decide on a title. Although the title should reflect the content of the paper, you can give it an interesting twist or perhaps make use of part of a quotation that seems particularly appropriate. Of course, there's nothing wrong with a straightforward title. In many cases, a no-nonsense title that gets straight to the point is your best choice.

Write an Introduction   The paper's premise serves as the basis of the introduction. In revising your paper, you can expand on this premise and come up with the introduction in its final form. In addition to stating your premise, the introduction explains how you plan to support it and can include an apt example, anecdote, or quotation. Choose any of these devices carefully; they must be right on target. If you're not sure they will contribute to the paper, then write a straightforward statement.

Bibliography

Carlson, Karen J., Eisenstat, Stephanie A., and Ziporyn, Terra, *The Harvard Guide to Women's Health.* Cambridge, Mass.: Harvard University Press, 1996.

Field, Shelly. *100 Best Careers for the 21st Century.* New York: Macmillan, 1996.

Hanke, Steve H. "The Stagnation Myth," *Forbes* 157 (April 22, 1996) 145–146.

Krefetz, Gerald. *Read and Profit from Financial News.* 2nd ed. Dearborn, Mich.: Dearborn Financial Publishing, Inc., 1995.

Maughan, Jackie Johnson, ed. *Go Tell It on the Mountain.* Mechanicsburg, Pa.: Stackpole Books, 1996.

Quammen, David. *The Song of the Dodo.* New York: Scribner, 1996.

Wertheimer, Neil, ed. *Total Health for Men.* Emmaus, Pa.: Rodale Press, 1995.

FIGURE A.6 Format for a Bibliography

State a Conclusion Don't end the paper without a concluding passage. If you do, your readers will be left dangling, wondering what happened to you and the rest of the paper. Let them know they have come to the end.

By now, all your major points should have been made and adequately supported. The primary purpose of your conclusion is to restate or summarize your basic premise. In addition, you may want to use your premise to draw a related conclusion. For example, if your premise states that alcohol is one of the country's leading causes of death and your paper has supported that contention with data and examples, you may want to conclude with some suggestions for dealing with the problem of alcohol abuse:

Taxes on alcoholic beverages should be increased.

Beer, wine, and liquor companies should be made to subsidize alcohol treatment programs.

Americans must overcome their tendency toward self-destructive addictive behavior.

Alcohol education should begin at the elementary school level.

Although the rest of your paper should be backed up with information you discovered through research, the conclusion affords you the opportunity to state your own opinion and draw a personal conclusion.

In general, of course, the kind of conclusion you write depends on the paper and the subject. In most cases, the conclusion need not be long and involved. But be certain you include one.

Keyboard the Final Copy

All the time and energy you have spent on your research paper should be reflected in the appearance of the final copy. Make it neat, clean, and attractive.

1. Use only one side of white paper. Although instructors seldom specify, most assume that your paper will be written on $8\frac{1}{2} \times 11$-inch sheets.
2. Leave a generous margin at the top and bottom of each page and a margin of $1\frac{1}{2}$ inches on both sides to provide room for the instructor's comments.
3. Type your paper or have it typed or word-processed. Of course, if you've written your paper on a computer, you can have it printed. Handwritten papers are difficult to read and may not even be accepted in some courses.
4. Set up long, direct quotations (of five or more lines) in block style—that is, single space and indent the lines from both sides about a half inch or five typewriter spaces. Omit the quotation marks when you block a quotation in this way—the block setup shows that you are quoting.
5. Proofread your final copy. Go over it carefully to catch spelling errors and other minor flaws. This is a very important step.

SUMMARY

How do you arrive at a research topic?	Start by selecting a general subject that interests you. Then narrow it down to a topic that's specific enough to cover in depth but large enough to allow you to find a sufficient amount of information. Finally, focus your topic by asking a question that gives your paper direction and purpose.
What sort of information should you look for, and where can you find it?	Look for books and magazine articles that deal with your specific topic. You can find them in the library by searching the card catalog (or computerized card catalog) for books and by consulting an index such as the *Reader's Guide* or Info-trac for magazine articles. If you get stuck in your search, ask a reference librarian for help.

How do you assemble a working bibliography?	Write the bibliographical information for each reference you plan to consult on the front of a 3 × 5 card. Use the back to summarize your opinion of each article or book.
How can you ensure that your notes are easy to use?	Jot each note on a separate 3 × 5 card. On each card, write the author and the page number of the source so you'll be able to verify the accuracy of your notes with ease and have all the information you need for citations. Use the modified printing style to write both quickly and neatly, and write in pen to prevent your notes from fading or smearing. Take concise but detailed notes. Use abbreviations for common words.
How can you ensure that your notes are accurate?	To ensure that the information in your notes is accurate, make a clear distinction among your own ideas, paraphrased information and quoted material. Copy quotations exactly as they appear in the source. If you shorten a quotation, insert an ellipsis in place of the words you've removed.
How do you decide on your paper's basic premise?	The premise for your paper can grow out of potential arguments, apparent similarities, or possible theories that you've developed from going over your notes.
How do you cluster your notes?	Select the note cards with the most important ideas you have jotted down, and then group the other notes beneath the idea they support. If a note doesn't support any of the main ideas, do not include it in your paper.
How do you plot out a pattern for your paper?	Use your premise as a starting point to organize your clusters of information into a logical pattern. Most college research papers follow one of three basic forms: the time pattern, the process pattern, or the development of an argument.
How should you write the first draft?	Speed, not style, is the key to completing your first draft. For now your goal is simply to get everything written down. Move systematically through your note cards, turning notes

into sentences and combining sentences into paragraphs.

How can you strengthen your paper's supporting material?	You can do so by double-checking your paragraphs to make sure that each idea is sufficiently developed. If an idea lacks support, bolster it with further explanation, data from authorities, statistics, or examples.
How do you fine-tune technical details?	Use transitional words and phrases to guide your reader through your paper. Make sure your grammar and spelling are correct. Consult an English handbook or a dictionary when in doubt.
What missing elements do you need to add?	You should include a citation for every reference you make, a bibliography of the sources you used, a title, an introduction, and a conclusion. These make your paper complete.
What are the requirements for the final copy?	Your final copy should be neat, clean, and attractive. Type or keyboard it carefully with generous margins, using only one side of each sheet of white paper, and double-check each page to make sure it is free of errors.

MY FIRST RESEARCH PAPER

By Walter Pauk

Registration was like a game of chess. The smart students made their moves early. Some lined up before dawn, while others used the university's new computerized system to register from home by telephone. They registered early, not especially to get the best courses, but to avoid being "stuck" with one—the one taught by Professor Wilbur Hendricon.

The word on the grapevine was that this was a course to be avoided by the faint of heart. The chances of being forced into Professor Hendricon's course were slim but still too terrifying to take a chance. Professor Hendricon had, as the students said, "a special deal with the administration." He could hand-pick twenty-five students for his class, but had to take another ten at general registration.

This unusual procedure was a compromise. It came about this way: Professor Hendricon had taught only graduate courses before; but ten years ago he decided that he would like to teach one section of English 105. So

Professor Hendricon suddenly proclaimed to the dean that he would take twenty-five first-year students and turn them into scholars.

The dean was faced with a dilemma. On the one hand, a negative answer might be taken as a rude rebuff by the proud and sensitive Hendricon. Also, the dean thought, "If he resigns, I will have to answer to the president." Hendricon was the university's brilliant light and he was eagerly sought after by other universities. On the other hand, a positive answer would be a blow to the morale of the other members of the English Department, who had no choice but to take their usual thirty-five students per class. The dean consulted her colleagues and persuaded them to accept the compromise. Needless to say, I was one of the unlucky ten.

Right from the very first day in class, I could see how well Hendricon had chosen. The twenty-five were geniuses. I later discovered that they all had straight As in high school and that they were clustered at the top of the scholarship list. Furthermore, they excelled in language and literature, while my strengths were in mathematics and music. Math skills and musical talent did not count for much in an English course.

At first I thought Professor Hendricon's legendary standards might just be rumor, but after the first test any hopes evaporated. We unfortunate ten compared notes and found our grades in the 30s and 40s. But no one questioned Professor Hendricon's honesty and sincerity. Our papers were filled with notations, symbols, and helpful comments. We did, however, question his standards. They were not for us mortals.

Six of the ten transferred to other sections of the course immediately; the other three students transferred after the second test. Everyone knew that transferring was possible. The other instructors expected to get all ten of us in their classes within the first few weeks of term. In this way morale was preserved, because administratively, at least, all the classes started out with thirty-five students each.

Perhaps it was the lemming instinct in me or perhaps it was Hendricon's appeal, but I decided to hang in. On the day after the last date for changing classes, I took my usual seat. The other twenty-five students, who usually chatted loudly until Professor Hendricon entered the door, were strangely silent today. You see, in all these past ten years, not one of the unchosen had ever stayed in Hendricon's class. Everyone knew this.

We could hear Hendricon's brisk but firm footsteps drawing closer to the open door. The pace was faster than usual. We saw the toe of his left foot puncture the blank space of the doorway. The blood was pounding at my temples. My breathing was fast and shallow. Hendricon always walked straight to the lectern, put down his notes, and said "good afternoon" to the class. As he entered today, he glanced at me with a curious look. He did not greet the class as usual. He just lectured, but more seriously. I could not keep my mind on the lecture. No one could. It seemed that I had spoiled the atmosphere of this select club. Why had I not been less foolhardy?

On Monday, however, the class resumed its normal pace and atmosphere. I was present but not accepted. The chosen twenty-five sat in a solid square. I sat outside the square, separate but linked like an appendix. But that did not bother me, for I was really fascinated by Professor Hendricon. He was a great teacher. I took copious notes and studied the assignments carefully. I occasionally forgot myself and spoke out during discussions. I worked hard on tests and examinations, but they were never quite up to standard. I could usually understand the ideas and concepts, but time always ran out. I needed more time to think. But I was not discouraged because I was enjoying the course and learning a lot.

It was just after the Christmas holidays that Professor Hendricon announced it. "It" was the research paper—3,500 words and counting for one-third of the final grade. I should have been petrified because I could not write, and yet, I was glad. This was my chance to raise my present hard-earned average of 62.7% to the necessary 70.

This would be the first instance where I would have an advantage over the students—I would have the advantage of time. I needed time. Time is the great equalizer; time is democratic. We all receive the same amount of it every morning. No distinction is made between the genius and the plodder. This is what I told myself; it helped me feel a little better.

There should not have been any excitement because everyone knew about the Hendricon paper. It was indeed another factor that encouraged the rush to register early for other courses. The paper was not due until after the late winter break—almost two months off. But still, there were groans and whisperings. I could hardly hear the professor's caution against plagiarism. "Use both the primary text as well as secondary critical sources," he instructed against a background of restless inattention. Very few paid attention to his next point about thinking carefully before choosing a topic. I somehow caught, "Once you have decided on your topic it should be narrowed three or four times." What did he mean by this?

After the others had left, I edged up to Professor Hendricon, who was gathering up his lecture notes, and asked about the idea of narrowing the topic. He said, "If, for example, you were doing a history course, and you chose as your topic the 'Civil War,' you would be almost sure to fail. You simply could not do justice to such a large topic—dozens of books would be necessary to cover that subject, not an undergraduate research paper. Even a second narrowing of the topic to the 'Battle of Gettysburg,' a major engagement in the war, would still be too broad. A third stage of narrowing such as the 'Battle of Cemetery Ridge' would be more manageable, but your focus might not be sufficiently defined yet. So perhaps a further narrowing to the 'Tactical Importance of Cemetery Ridge' might be necessary. This would be an aspect of the original broad topic on which adequate information could be found to write an in-depth paper."

I was so excited about writing the term paper that I went straight to the library eager and determined to find an interesting topic on which to use this technique of narrowing. I was surprised to find the cavernous library so empty of students. But of course, there would be time during "reading week" and the late winter break—there was no pressure yet. I went directly to the reference librarian who showed me how to use the various special reference books. Another librarian, who joined us, had an interesting idea. She said, "If you choose a subject area carefully in your first year, and continue throughout your university years to research and write in that area, you could probably become quite an expert." This idea intrigued me.

Over the next few days I brainstormed possible topics for my paper. First, I scrutinized Professor Hendricon's course outline, mulling over his lecture themes and the prescribed authors and texts. Then I returned to the library to peruse reference books such as encyclopedias, surveys of literature, and biographical dictionaries. I developed a list of nineteen topics that interested me. I reflected on these over the weekend and after careful deliberation rejected fourteen of them.

The remaining five topics I decided to discuss with Professor Hendricon. He seemed happy to see me. In about five minutes we eliminated two. As far as the other three were concerned, he suggested that I talk about each with professors who were experts in the respective areas.

These talks were especially stimulating. I got to know three new professors from whom I received not only useful insights about narrowing the topics but also details of important sources and prominent authorities as well. After thinking through the suggestions made by these professors. I settled on the area that was most appealing to me.

I arranged another session with Professor Hendricon to inform him of my decision and to obtain advice on the direction my assignment should take. We discussed the precise purpose of my paper, and, over a cup of tea, we juggled words and finally formulated a challenging question to launch my research. I emerged from his Dickensian study aglow with inspiration and enthusiasm. The stern and serious Hendricon of the lecture hall had a warm and sensitive side that few students had glimpsed.

So, with the topic narrowed and a clear sense of direction established, back to the library I went to search for sources and to start my research. With the first week over I was surprised to find none of the class in the library. During the first term I had learned how to use the library's computerized catalogue. Why not explore other searching opportunities offered by the computer system, such as using a key word to locate titles relevant to the focus of my research? I was amazed at the wealth of material available through the computer catalogue, and soon I had an impressive list of titles in my working bibliography. Gaining confidence, I decided to use the CD-ROM databases and discovered a number of periodical articles pertaining to my research question.

I gathered some of my sources and began taking notes on pages of paper. The reference librarian, ever helpful, wandered over and asked if I knew the advantages of recording my notes on 3 × 5 slips. Without waiting for an answer, she said that the ability to categorize my notes would ensure a much more efficient research system. Her specific suggestions were these:

- Record only one point, or a small cluster of related points, on one card.

- Record only information that is relevant to the purpose of your research.

- Use only one side of the card.

- Each card should indicate the author and page numbers of the source.

- Enclose all verbatim notes in quotation marks.

- Most notes should be paraphrased or summarized.

- Whenever you have a thought or insight of your own, jot it down and enclose it with brackets to signify "my own."

Noticing that I had no slips, she darted to her desk and pulled out the bottom drawer and thumped several rubber-banded stacks of cards on my table. "These are old cards left over when we converted the catalogue to a computer system. They are only used on one side. You are welcome to use them for your research notes."

The card method intrigued me and now that I had a wide-ranging list of sources, I was anxious to get started on the research. I worked steadily in the library for the next two weeks, averaging two to three hours a day. It was surprisingly easy jotting down important information and ideas on cards and indicating the sources and page numbers. Rather than waste time writing out the author's name or the title on each card, I used a simple coding system to identify each source. I did not have a written outline. I had tried to prepare one after formulating my question, but I could not anticipate the material I would find. I also sensed that it would be too restricting. However, although I did not have an outline, it would be unfair to say that I selected the material for my note cards haphazardly. I selected material that had a bearing on my specific question. Once I immersed myself in the research, I began to sense what was relevant and what was not.

After two weeks, I had a shoebox full of cards. I was ready to start structuring and drafting the paper. During the course of the research I had sketched out a tentative list of sections that might serve as an outline. I stepped back from my intense two-week spell of research to reflect on the provisional outline. Keeping the research question uppermost in my mind, I modified the sections so that they would provide a structure around which I could shape my answer. Next, I read through all my note cards and moved them into categories corresponding to my outline. Having notes on each card that pertained to only one idea permitted me to place the cards in separate categories. If I had put two different notes on one card, I would have had to rewrite the information onto two separate cards now. I was glad that I had a system. It was like playing cards.

My outline required further modification because not all the cards fitted the major sections. I added another section to accommodate some of the cards, while a number of cards simply did not fit into any of the sections. So, with the cards in categories, I started to follow the second step of the librarian's advice. I began to shift the piles of cards into an order that seemed logical for my paper. It was surprisingly easy to re-order the piles of cards so that there was a logical flow in the sequence of the sections.

With the categories of cards spread out before me, I began to study each category independently to create a detailed outline. As I wrestled with sections, subsections and supporting material I began to see where I had gaps in data and weak spots in the argument. My detailed outline revealed plainly the areas in which my paper lacked balance and completeness. My work was cut out for the next few days since I needed specifics that the paper presently lacked. I was glad that each card carried a reference to the source, so that I could locate not only the source but the precise page as well.

After a few hours of additional research in the library, I was able to augment my note cards. I felt that the more complete I could make my collection of cards, the more effective the first draft would be. I remembered Professor Hendricon's advice: "If you do not gather enough first-class material, you will have trouble writing a major paper." I used some of the new research information to revise and refine my detailed outline.

Finally, I was satisfied with my outline. Then I began to write the first draft. It surprised me to see how easy it is to write a long paper once the material is placed in order. I actually enjoyed the process. It took four days of writing in my spare time to complete the draft. I preferred writing my first draft in longhand because I seemed to think more clearly when writing rather than typing. On each day, I concentrated on writing one of four major parts of the paper. When I had finished, I immediately read it over and it sounded good to me—so good that I knew I would be able to enjoy the late-winter holidays. A wonderful reward. First, I had to type up my draft on the computer, and after saving it carefully on the hard drive, I took the floppy disk over to the computer center and printed a copy. I proudly left the copy on my desk to cool while I went home for the holidays.

On the last day before we departed for our week's holiday, Professor Hendricon did his duty as a teacher to remind us to work on our papers because they were due five days after our return to campus. The students fidgeted, a nervous laugh or two mingled with some of the spontaneous whispering, but no one said anything. I thought to myself that I had not seen any of the chosen twenty-five in the library; but then they could have been there at other times. Also, the thought struck me that they loved to discuss every moot point and debate hypothetical issues. They seemed to excel at writing creative papers, often at the last minute, with information they already had in their heads. Perhaps a research paper that demanded hard and dogged work was just too rigorous for their creative souls. Well, I just thought these thoughts and was a bit ashamed at my suspicious mind.

Even though I was still failing Professor Hendricon's course, the warm feeling generated by my completed draft provided the tone that I needed to enjoy my holidays. I had a good rest.

I arrived back on campus on Friday to avoid the weekend traffic. That evening, feeling proud of myself, I casually picked up my draft and, to extract the maximum amount of satisfaction from my accomplishment, I began reading. By the time I had finished page 3, my smile had vanished, and by page 10 fear had gripped me. The development of my thesis, which sounded so smooth upon completion, was now disjointed and repetitious and some paragraphs were meaningless. How could that be?

I pacified myself after the initial shock by realizing that I still had seven days, while many of the other students in the class had not even started their papers. Most of them would only arrive back on campus on Sunday evening, and that would leave them but a scant five days. As I pondered how to fix up my research paper, I realized for the first time, the truth of the words that I had discarded as "teachers' preachings": "No paper should ever be handed in unless you have revised it. For the revision to be effective, you must always put your paper away for a few days so that you will lose some familiarity with it. Then, when you reread it, you will be better able to spot the weaknesses and the rough sections. Once these are spotted, revise, revise, revise."

My paper was certainly rough. I recalled the steps for revising: first look through the draft to make sure the ideas are understandable and supported by details and examples. Second, make sure the organizational plan for the paper is clear and that the sections are in logical sequence. Third, check for consistency of style, and, finally, ensure that the mechanics such as spelling and hyphenating are correct. I discovered that I had scattered throughout the paper bits of interesting information—interesting but not always pertinent. I added some of the misplaced material to the introduction and eliminated the rest. It was tough to throw away these gems that I had worked so hard to extract from my sources, but I heard ringing in my ears: "Good writers don't put everything down that is interesting. Remember the iceberg with its nine-tenths underwater and only one-tenth showing above the surface. This submerged part—your background work—gives the iceberg its strength and power."

After weeding out the irrelevant material, I concentrated on the structure of the paper and discovered that it, too, was a bit vague. Parts of the general statement that should have been at the beginning were in the body of the paper. So I sharpened the introduction by stating the thesis and then broke it down to the five main points that I had planned to establish and support. By the time I had reworked the introduction, I really knew for the first time what I was attempting to do. I was shocked to realize that my own understanding of what I was trying to do had not been clear. By the time I went to sleep on Sunday, I had hammered out a clear statement of what I was trying to establish and support.

Monday rolled around all too soon. The vacation was over. There was a lot of activity on campus as students accelerated into a faster tempo of study. Papers were due, final examinations hovered on the horizon, and most plans to complete work during the holidays had fallen through. Hendricon reminded the class of the Friday deadline. There was no whispering this time, just grim silence. I, too, contributed to the silence. I had to write not only a passing paper, but a paper good enough to earn an 85 if I was to raise my average to the passing grade of 70. I had, perhaps, counted too heavily on time and technique. Time was running out and technique was not holding up. But I still had a chance. Most of the chosen twenty-five, I was sure, had not even started.

I worked hard to strengthen the body of the paper by realigning my main sections in the same order as in the statement of thesis in the introduction. I made sure that each main section led off with a brief paragraph that introduced the section. Then I grouped the supporting information in a number of separate paragraphs all focused on the central idea of the section. As I worked through the other sections checking the paragraph structure, I was surprised to discover that some of the supporting materials were still widely scattered even though I had carefully laid out a sequence when I grouped my note cards. By moving some of the information to more appropriate sections, I was able to eliminate repetition. I reworked each main section, especially those that seemed vague or hastily composed. Occasionally, I dug back into my collection of note cards when an idea needed additional support.

On Tuesday I fashioned a concluding summary that was not repetitious, synthesizing the thesis and key points in such a way to show mastery of the material. After dinner I took my disk over to the computer center and printed a copy of the complete paper. I was immensely relieved and satisfied when I fell asleep that evening.

After the 9 o'clock class on Wednesday, I was free to devote the whole day to the final editing of the essay. I first read the entire paper aloud, checking for style. By reading aloud I could better detect redundant words, vague phrases, and awkward sounding sentences. I corrected the flawed sentences so that they flowed smoothly and naturally. As part of the editing process, I made frequent use of a dictionary and a thesaurus to ensure that the vocabulary was precise. Also, I worked on internal transitions to give my paragraphs and sentences better cohesion. After I had edited the printed copy, I corrected the computer version and saved it carefully. I was meticulous in backing up copies on diskette in the event my computer malfunctioned.

I woke early on Thursday excited to see the final copy in print at last. I rushed down to the computer room after breakfast and printed out my "magnum opus." I was so anxious to start proofreading that I toyed with the possibility of skipping my morning lectures. But with final examinations looming, common sense won out! After lectures, I gobbled my lunch down and headed for my room and my prized paper. I proofread it meticulously, from title page to bibliography. All my thoroughness had paid off—not a single error was apparent. I was flushed with that warm feeling of satisfaction that the completion of a creative assignment brings.

This was it. This was the day! I never heard such an outpouring of incidents to a professor from frantic, frightened students who tried so hard to look and act sophisticated. "The library is so full, you can't find a table to write on." "Two other students are working on the same topic as I am and I cannot get hold of the sources." "My computer crashed." "My printer overheated and seized up." "I'll need more time, because all the typists in town are busy, and they can't get to mine until after the weekend."

Hendricon was calm but exceedingly serious. He looked around the room solemnly, making no attempt to answer any of the excuses. After a moment, he held up his hand for quiet and went on with his lecture as if nothing had happened. There was deep silence that hour. Professor Hendricon was always good, but he was especially good that day. He talked hard and earnestly. Most of the students sat glumly, motionless and glassy-eyed. Only a few had the discipline to take notes. For some reason, the professor's words seemed to be aimed at me. He was trying to make scholars of us, as well as mature men and women. About half the students handed in papers that day. Spurred by the announcement, "Five points a day will be deducted on all late papers," the rest were in on the following Monday. I was pleased and proud that mine was in on time.

With only two and a half weeks to go, Professor Hendricon lectured hard and fast, determined to complete his schedule of lectures. By now, I had reconciled myself that failure was a possibility. Though I still wanted to pass the course, I was not too worried about it. I was just glad to have had the opportunity to attend Professor Hendricon's class.

On the last day of class, Professor Hendricon strode in with our research papers. "Before I hand them back to you," he said, "I want to talk about them both generally and specifically." He continued, "A few of the papers were excellent, a few poor, and the majority mediocre. The excellent ones were creative and imaginative in their use of technique; but the poor ones seemed as if they had been put together artificially and mechanically with scissors and paste."

That last remark hit me. Of course, I should have known that Professor Hendricon would be quick to see the artificial way my paper was put together: how I took notes on cards; distributed them in piles; mechanically shifted stacks of cards around; made an outline last, not first; filled gaps by digging out more material; mechanically revised, looked up words, read aloud to detect faulty intonation—all done like a "hack" in mechanical and piecemeal fashion. The rest of the class had real talent—they were truly gifted. In four or five days, they were able to write down their thoughts directly, fully developed, like true artists. And like true artists, they made good with one chance, whereas I had dozens of chances to write and rewrite.

As Professor Hendricon continued to talk about "scissors and paste," he suddenly picked up a paper to illustrate a point. I was shocked. I could tell it was my paper. I just couldn't stand the embarrassment. All I wanted to do was to get out of that room, fast! Then I suddenly realized that though I knew it was my paper, no one else did. So I steeled myself. Professor Hendricon read one paragraph after another. He jumped to the first part of the paper for a paragraph, then to the end for another. Then I noticed that the rest of the class was listening attentively, and though Professor Hendricon's voice was excited, it was kindly. As I calmed and composed myself, I heard, "Note the smooth rhythm of the prose and the careful choice of words. This is what I mean by scholarship. The technique is discernible. Yes! But put together with a scholar's love, and care, and time."

P.S. You guessed it! I passed the course.

HAVE YOU MISSED SOMETHING?

Sentence Completion

Complete the following sentences with one of the three words or phrases listed below each sentence.

1. Give your research purpose, direction, and focus by developing a
    _____ about your topic.
       scientific discovery   fascinating misconception
       compelling question

2. When you are using the computerized magazine indexes of a library, a Boolean search enables you to narrow your search by
_____ .

using a prominent key word   combining two key words
using a full sentence

3. As you discover magazines and books that relate to your research, add them to a working bibliography that is _____ .
in your notebook   on separate 3 × 5 cards   on separate 5 × 8 cards

Matching

In each blank space in the left column, write the letters preceding the phrase in the right column that matches the left item best.

_____ 1. Compelling question
_____ 2. *Reader's Guide*
_____ 3. Abstract
_____ 4. Index
_____ 5. Ellipsis
_____ 6. Concept map
_____ 7. Preliminary research
_____ 8. Library

a. Can help you find a suitable topic
b. Synopsis found at the beginning of some journal articles
c. Can be used to visually plan your paper
d. Helps provide a focus for your paper
e. Primary source for most of your paper's information
f. Good starting point in the search for books or magazines
g. Best-known index of periodicals
h. Indicates that part of a quotation has been omitted

True-False

Write *T* beside the *true* statements and *F* beside the *false* statements.

_____ 1. Three or four narrowings should reduce your general topic to a suitable size.

_____ 2. A working bibliography consists of only those references you cited in your paper.

_____ 3. Info-trac is an example of a computerized magazine index.

_____ **4.** Like a card catalog, a computerized catalog enables you to search by subject, author, or title.

_____ **5.** A "cooling off" period is helpful between the writing of your first draft and your second draft.

_____ **6.** Paraphrasing is permitted in a research paper.

_____ **7.** A conclusion isn't always necessary in a research paper.

Multiple Choice

Choose the phrase that completes each of the following sentences most accurately, and circle the letter that precedes it.

1. The basic skills for writing a research paper are similar to those for
   a. writing a novel or short story.
   b. preparing for a test or quiz.
   c. taking notes during a lecture.
   d. doing none of the above.

2. The most common criticism of research papers is that they are
   a. too broad.
   b. too long.
   c. poorly written.
   d. carelessly researched.

3. The *Reader's Guide* is a common example of a
   a. Boolean search.
   b. style manual.
   c. periodical index.
   d. card catalog.

4. A research librarian is an expert on
   a. most research paper topics.
   b. the proper form for footnotes.
   c. use of the library.
   d. all the above.

5. Your notes will be easier to use if you
    a. recopy them so they are easy to read.
    b. copy all your information verbatim.
    c. jot down each note on a separate index card.
    d. fit them on as few pages as possible.

6. In writing your first draft, you should emphasize
    a. speed.
    b. accuracy.
    c. style.
    d. neatness.

7. You can avoid the appearance of plagiarism by including
    a. quotation marks.
    b. citations.
    c. a bibliography.
    d. all the above.

Short Answer

Supply a brief answer for each of the following items.

1. List some of the advantages and disadvantages of a computerized magazine index.

2. How can Boolean searching be used to pinpoint references?

3. How can concept maps be used in organizing a research paper?

Vocabulary Building

Directions: Make a light check mark (✓) alongside one of the three words (choices) that most nearly expresses the meaning of the italicized word in the phrases that are in the left-hand column. (Answers are given on page 97.)

		1	**2**	**3**
1.	*brevity* is the secret	seriousness	lengthiness	briefness
2.	jot down your *assessment*	appointment	function	evaluation
3.	to *counteract* forgetting	overcome	promote	reinforce
4.	trying to *decipher*	encode	decode	rewrite
5.	use three *ellipsis* points	spherical	orbital	periods
6.	*delve* into books	grow	probe	put away
7.	clearly and *forcibly*	predictably	lightly	powerfully
8.	it isn't *infallible*	unreliable	certain	refutable
9.	as *blatant* as copying	obvious	inconspicuous	easy
10.	*cite* your source	condemn	reveal	conceal
11.	grounds for *expulsion*	exclusion	acceptance	imitation
12.	the paper's *premise*	predicament	preposition	position
13.	an apt *example*	incongruity	illustration	argument
14.	*scanning* the bookshelves	browsing	measuring	arranging
15.	*relatively* recent entries	absolutely	comparably	similarly
16.	computer *terminals*	stations	openings	assignments
17.	if you *paraphrase*	recant	quote	reword
18.	*subsequent* research	following	previous	successful
19.	the wallop is *ineluctable*	unavoidable	probable	unexpected
20.	it *portends* a decline	rejects	foretells	invites
21.	and his *colleagues*	associates	competitors	investors
22.	*blighted* housing projects	improved	promoted	withered
23.	*loath* to see	eager	reluctant	enthusiastic
24.	streak of *defiance*	resistance	gratitude	determination
25.	mapping *contingency* plans	emergency	continuing	corporate

Additional Multiple-Choice Questions

1. If you need some help in choosing your paper topic, you can
   a. consult the *Reader's Guide to Periodical Literature.*
   b. ask a librarian for assistance.
   c. scan the bookshelves in your area of interest.
   d. do all the above.

2. The best way to arrive at a suitable topic for a research paper is to
   a. select a topic that is listed in the library catalog.
   b. put your subject through three significant narrowings.
   c. pick a subject that has a limited number of references.
   d. refer to old research papers for a workable idea.

3. Like the traditional card catalogue, the computerized catalog
   a. allows you to search for a book by author, subject, or title.
   b. contains information that is only of interest to librarians.
   c. requires you to scan a long list of names or titles.
   d. is updated by the library on a daily basis.

4. You can make your notes easier to use by
   a. taking them on separate 3 × 5 cards or slips of paper.
   b. identifying each one with the author or title of the source it came from.
   c. marking the specific page on which you located the information.
   d. doing all the above.

5. The basic premise is
   a. a theory that influences the way you do your research.
   b. the statement that provides the key evidence for your argument.
   c. the fundamental approach that underlies your paper.
   d. a transition that moves you smoothly from paragraph to paragraph.

6. In most cases, a research paper should cover fewer than
   a. ten main ideas.
   b. four main ideas.
   c. seven main ideas.
   d. three main ideas.

7. The organizational pattern of your paper will be influenced by
   a. personal choice.
   b. your basic premise.
   c. the available patterns.
   d. all the above.

8. The best way to start writing your research paper is to
   a. warm up with a detailed introduction.
   b. "brainstorm" the key points you want to begin with.
   c. simply begin writing.
   d. do all the above.

9. All the main points in your paper should be
   a. backed up with expert opinion.
   b. illustrated with memorable examples.
   c. adequately supported.
   d. linked with generalities.

10. Plagiarism is
     a. stealing.
     b. using another writer's ideas without giving credit.
     c. incorporating quoted material without citing it.
     d. all the above.

ANSWERS FOR WRITING A RESEARCH PAPER

Sentence Completion

1. compelling question   2. combining two key words   3. on separate 3 × 5 cards

Matching

1. d   2. g   3. b   4. f   5. h   6. c   7. a   8. e

True-False

1. T   2. F   3. T   4. T   5. T   6. T   7. F

Multiple Choice

1. b   2. a   3. c   4. c   5. c   6. a   7. d

Vocabulary Building

1. 3   2. 3   3. 1   4. 2   5. 3   6. 2   7. 3   8. 2   9. 1   10. 2   11. 1   12. 3   13. 2
14. 1   15. 2   16. 1   17. 3   18. 1   19. 1   20. 2   21. 1   22. 3   23. 2   24. 1
25. 1

Additional Multiple-Choice Questions

1. d   2. b   3. a   4. d   5. c   6. c   7. d   8. c   9. c   10. d

The whole of science is nothing more than a refinement of everyday thinking.

ALBERT EINSTEIN

(1879–1955), German-American physicist, formulator of the special theory of relativity

Supplementary Chapter B

STUDYING SCIENCE

KENNETH GREISEN

Science has been called the endless frontier, but for some students it seems just plain endless. There are endless lectures, endless textbooks, endless problems, endless labs. This chapter presents some techniques to help make science a little less intimidating and a little more exciting. It provides effective methods for

- Learning from lectures
- Reading a science textbook
- Working scientific problems
- Working in the laboratory

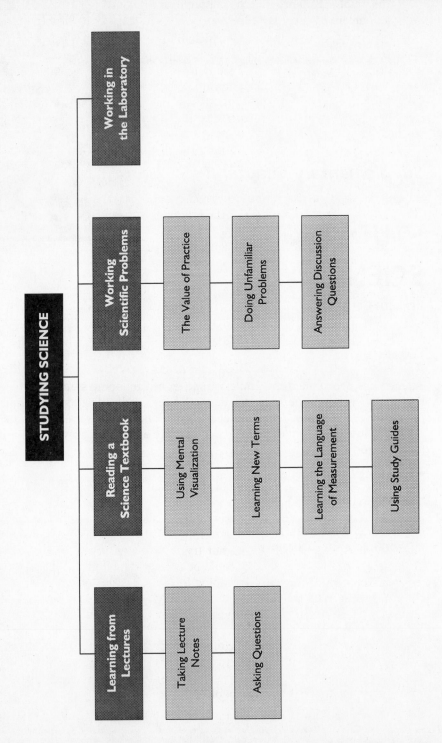

In every subject that you study, including science, you must learn new terminology, facts, and ideas; then you must develop the ability to apply them to solve various problems. Studying science, however, is different from studying other subjects. First, the terminology, facts, laws, and principles must be learned with extreme precision. Second, the problems are almost always quantitative, and most of the ideas are stated in quantitative (mathematical) terms.

A good example is the definition of *work*, which is learned early in the study of physics: The work W done by a force of magnitude F in moving a body through a distance d in the direction of the force is $W = F \times d$. For a student who is unaccustomed to precise and quantitative terms, such a definition can be intimidating, for the following reasons:

1. The definition is precise, and it must be learned and used precisely. What might seem like a minor rewording could render the definition incorrect and thus useless.
2. The definition contains several parts, and the reasoning underlying each part must be understood if the definition as a whole is to be understood.
3. The definition is quantitative. It makes use of a formula to define *work*, and that formula may be used to calculate work under certain conditions.
4. The student must learn what those conditions are and how to take them into account when using the formula.
5. The scientific meaning of the word *work* is different from the meaning we're used to. Other common words also have special meanings in the sciences; in such cases, the everyday definitions can get in the way of remembering the scientific definitions.

The reason for this degree of precision is that the sciences deal with actual, measurable things. If these things are not described or computed precisely, they will not be described or computed correctly.

You need to learn the precise terminology, facts, and ideas when you study a science. But you should not try to learn a science as if it were a collection of isolated facts. That would be an almost impossible task, and the isolated facts would have little meaning for you. The way to learn science is to fit facts and principles together into groups, or clusters, in your memory. Within each science, facts and principles are related to one another to a much greater extent than in nonscientific subjects, so clustering should be easier.

Actually, much of science is concerned with finding and explaining the relationships among various facts, concepts, and theories. Even our precise definition of *work* is really a relationship; it is given as a formula because the relation is a precise one. Your textbook and teachers will point out many more.

Your job is to use these relationships to cluster the factors and ideas in your mind.

As you learn in this way, your knowledge of a few facts in a cluster will easily extend to new facts and ideas that you want to include in the same cluster. You will find yourself becoming more and more comfortable with science and its precision. You may begin to ask yourself questions about how new ideas fit in with old ones, about the patterns that you find in both old and new facts, or about why a principle that you learned in one science course seems so much like a principle you learned in another. Then you will really be learning science.

LEARNING FROM LECTURES

Your objective is to learn the facts and their interrelationships, and your ears and eyes must be alert to both. Take full, legible notes during lectures, paying particular attention to explanatory diagrams. Don't hesitate to ask questions if you cannot grasp a point after reviewing your lecture notes and reading your text.

Taking Lecture Notes

You should take science lecture notes and study them in the manner described in Chapter 10.

Taking Notes on Ideas   Do not try to take down the lecture word for word. If you do, the words will get in the way of the ideas. The objective of taking notes is to have a record of the main ideas so that you can study them later for deeper understanding, for review, and for examinations.

Being Systematic   Use the Cornell System for taking notes. The format is shown in Figure B.1. Write your notes in the right-hand column. Then, as soon as possible after each lecture, put your notes in order by filling in missing steps in the arguments, by correcting errors, and by relating these new notes with the previous lecture's notes. Label each idea on the right with a question, placed in the narrow left-hand column.

Making Master Summary Sheets   Periodically (to prepare for tests or at regular intervals), reorganize your notes on separate sheets of paper by clustering the ideas and details under main topics and categories. By con-

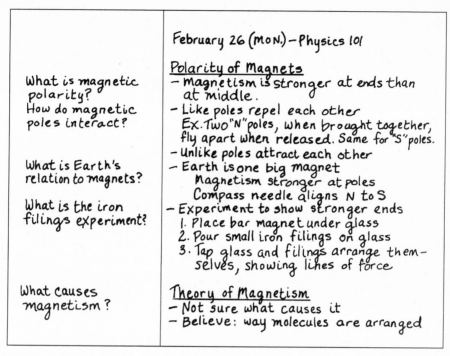

FIGURE B.1   Cornell System Format for Lecture Notes and Notes Based on Textbook Reading

structing summary sheets, you will be relating facts and ideas to one another and fixing them in your memory.

Asking Questions

If you have trouble relating concepts, solving assigned problems, or completing lab experiments satisfactorily, there may be gaps in your understanding. In such cases, you should ask questions.

Asking the Teacher at the Start of the Class   The start of the class is usually the best time to ask questions. Well-phrased questions about the previous lecture or the reading assignment can often be cleared up quickly. Moreover, something that presented difficulty for you probably did the same for other members of the class; your teacher may want to discuss the troublesome area during the lecture.

Never worry or feel embarrassed about being the only student who doesn't understand something or about showing that you didn't grasp a particular idea. If you do, you will be underestimating the teacher and yourself, misjudging the purpose of the course, and making it hard for the teacher to keep in touch with the class. Don't, however, ask questions like "How do you do this problem?" Such a question may get you the answer to the problem, but it will do little to increase your understanding. Much better questions are "Did I use the right strategy in attacking this problem? Are there other strategies that I could have used?" Such questions will get you useful information—ideas that you can apply to a broad range of material.

Interrupting a Lecture   Don't be bashful; interrupt a lecture with a question if you need to. Often it is helpful for the whole class to have a lecture slowed down or brought to a halt for a while—especially if some point is obscure. But don't interrupt too often, and make sure your question is important to you.

Asking the Teacher Between Classes   A good teacher's interest in his or her subject and students continues between classes in spite of many other duties. Most teachers enjoy a discussion with an individual student. But remember one thing: Before asking for assistance, do (or at least try) the assignment and think about the problems for yourself. Private sessions with your teacher should only supplement your own work. The major part of learning must be done by you alone.

Asking Other Students   Discussions with other students can be a great help. Friends learning a subject together often share the same difficulties and can thus enlighten one another very effectively.

READING A SCIENCE TEXTBOOK

In some ways, studying a science textbook is like studying any other textbook. You should take notes using the Cornell format, review them using the recitation method, and from time to time make master summary sheets.

Different sciences, however, call for different attacks and emphases in your reading. Generally, biology and geology place relatively heavy emphasis on key terms and definitions; physics and astronomy, on measurement and mathematics; biology and chemistry, on manipulation; and physics and chemistry, on visualization. Make sure you adapt your study methods accordingly. There are some special techniques that you should use to get the most out of your science textbook. For example, you should keep in mind that science texts are packed with information. You must read them sentence by sentence, making sure you understand each sentence before going on to the next one. Here are four more techniques.

Using Mental Visualization

James Clerk Maxwell (1831–1879), a Scottish mathematical physicist, recognized that different people, as they read and study science, mentally visualize or reconstruct concepts and ideas in their own personal ways. He believed that the concepts and ideas of science can be lifted out of a textbook and placed in one's mind only by the process of mental visualization. Maxwell also believed that although people have different ways of visualizing, everyone does it to varying degrees.

Fortunately, most textbooks and articles in science are heavily illustrated with diagrams to aid the process of visualization. Learn to use the illustrations and text in such a way that they complement one another. When there is no diagram to illustrate a process or an idea, or if a given diagram doesn't work for you, then make your own. This technique is discussed and illustrated in Chapter 13.

Learning New Terms

Your science textbooks contain many terms that are new to you. Because these terms stand for essential concepts, you must know precisely what they mean if you are to understand the subject matter. To help you pick out important new terms, textbooks usually emphasize them by means of italic or bold type when they first occur. Such terms are specifically defined at that point or in a glossary at the end of the book. Give extra time and attention to the task of memorizing these terms and their definitions. Jot them down on 3 × 5 cards, and master each one as you would any new word.

Learning the Language of Measurement

Learning the language of scientific measurement is important. Most commonly used are the metric system and the Celsius and Fahrenheit temperature scales. Learn to think meaningfully about these quantities and measures.

You should know that the word *metric* comes from *meter*, which is the principal unit of length in this system. The metric system was developed by French scientists in 1799 and is now used everywhere in the world for scientific work. Table B.1 compares some metric units with English units of measurement.

TABLE B.1 Comparison of Metric and English Units

Metric System			English System		
		Length			
Meter	=	1.093 yards	Avoirdupois	=	0.9144 meter
	=	3.281 feet	Foot	=	0.3048 meter
	=	39.370 inches	Inch	=	0.0254 meter
Kilometer	=	0.621 mile	Mile	=	1.609 kilometers
		Weight			
Gram	=	15.432 grains	Grain	=	0.0648 gram
	=	0.032 troy ounce	Troy ounce	=	31.1 grams
	=	0.0352 avoirdupois ounce	Avoirdupois		
Kilogram	=	2.2046 pounds avoirdupois	ounce	=	28.35 grams
Metric ton	=	2204.62 pounds avoirdupois	Pound	=	453.6 grams
Carat	=	3.08 grains avoirdupois	Short ton	=	0.907 metric ton

You will also want to know about the Celsius and Fahrenheit temperature scales. The thermometers for both look alike, have the same size tubes, and are filled with mercury that rises and falls to the same levels. But Celsius and Fahrenheit thermometers differ in the way their respective scales are graduated. On the Celsius thermometer, the point at which water freezes is marked 0 (zero); on the Fahrenheit thermometer scale it is marked 32. And on the Celsius scale, the boiling point of water is 100; on the Fahrenheit scale, it is 212.

On the Celsius thermometer, there are 100 equal spaces or degrees between the freezing and boiling points of water. On the Fahrenheit thermometer, there are 180 degrees between the freezing and boiling points. To change Celsius readings to Fahrenheit readings, multiply the Celsius reading by 180/100, or 9/5, and then add 32. To change Fahrenheit readings to Celsius readings, subtract 32 from the Fahrenheit reading and then multiply by 5/9.

Using Study Guides

Study guides accompany the textbooks for many science courses. One type of guide uses what is called a *programmed* approach. In this approach, a section of the guide containing sentence-completion questions corresponds to each section of the textbook. The questions help you evaluate what you've learned and what you still need to review. They also help you rehearse for examinations. In addition, there is a brief summary of each chapter and a list of chapter objectives. The value of the summary is self-evident. And the objectives constitute a ready-made self-test that you can use to make sure you've learned the important concepts in the chapter.

A second type of study guide contains, for each textbook chapter, the following items: an overview, chapter objectives, expanded chapter outline, student study objectives, vocabulary checklist, and self-tests. When using this type of guide, you should read the text chapter *before* attending the lecture on that chapter. Then, after the lecture, read the overview, objectives, and outline in the guide, and summarize the chapter in your own words. Check through the student study objectives, and write out any answers that are called for. Next, make sure you can define all the terms in the vocabulary checklist. Finally, take the self-tests to check that you have mastered the chapter. Use the study guide along with your notes when you review for an examination.

WORKING SCIENTIFIC PROBLEMS

The Value of Practice

Never skip an assigned practice problem. The most successful way to solve a problem on a test is to remember how you solved a similar problem previously. When you first attempt a new kind of problem, it is natural to be hesitant, to make false starts, to be stumped temporarily—to waste time. But as you work other problems of the same kind, you learn to do them quickly and surely. Because each problem usually has a feature not present in previous ones, you gradually develop the ability to solve a wider and wider range of problems.

Complex problems are usually solved in a series of simple steps. If the steps are so familiar that you do them automatically, you can concentrate on how they fit together to produce a solution to the problem. Then you can proceed from start to finish without confusion. However, if each step is difficult for you, you'll be so involved in details that you won't find the right path to the solution.

In studying a science, therefore, you should do more than just the assigned problems. If your own textbook does not have many extras, look for problems in other books on the same subject, or try to make up appropriate problems for yourself. Making up good problems is hard, but it is an excellent exercise—particularly for two students who are studying together. If you do this, try to anticipate the sorts of problems your teacher will make up for your tests.

Doing Unfamiliar Types of Problems

If you do your assignments faithfully, you will come across new and unfamiliar problems in your homework. Try to approach such problems in this way:

1. Don't start doing problems until you have studied your lecture and textbook notes.
2. Make a list of what is given in the problem and what is to be found.
3. Try to develop a chain of logical steps leading either forward from the known quantities to the unknown you have to find, or backward from the unknown to the given quantities. If necessary, work from both ends to the middle until you find a logical connection.
4. Express these logical steps in the form of equations.
5. Combine the equations and solve them for the unknown.
6. Check your answer by determining whether it is reasonable in magnitude. If you are unsure, substitute the answer into the original relations and see whether it fits consistently.

Answering Discussion Questions

Discussion questions appear occasionally in quizzes and examinations. Before you answer one, try to understand the purpose and point of view of the person asking the question. Learn to put yourself mentally in his or her place. Ask yourself how the question is related to subjects that were recently discussed in class or in your reading assignments and what principles it is intended to illustrate. If you can visualize the question within your clusters of facts and ideas, you'll be able to determine how you want to answer it. All that remains is to express your answer clearly, using the technical words accurately.

You need practice to become skillful in answering discussion questions. You can develop this skill by taking part in discussions with your friends, by participating in classroom discussions, and by paying careful attention to your *writing* skills. Usually your difficulties will be not in grammar but in vocabulary, in logic, and in ordering the steps in an argument.

WORKING IN THE LABORATORY

Here are seven hints for laboratory work:

1. *Do not trust your memory.* Write down everything you think may be pertinent. Some things that you observe in the laboratory may seem so

memorable at the time that you see no point in writing them down. But memory fades; if you do not write up an experiment completely when you perform it, you may not be able to recall important items. Figures B.2 and B.3 show the types of items that you should note immediately.

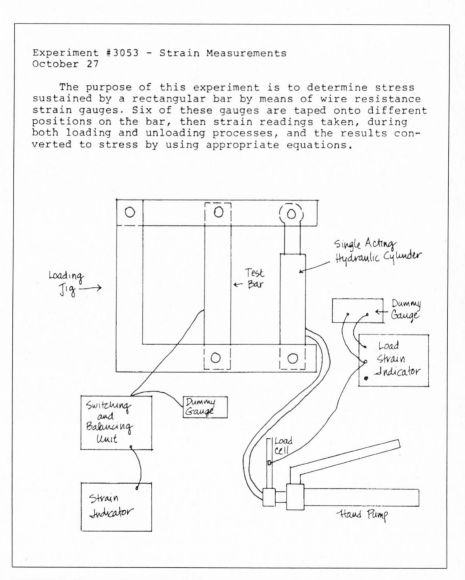

Experiment #3053 - Strain Measurements
October 27

    The purpose of this experiment is to determine stress sustained by a rectangular bar by means of wire resistance strain gauges. Six of these gauges are taped onto different positions on the bar, then strain readings taken, during both loading and unloading processes, and the results converted to stress by using appropriate equations.

FIGURE B.2   Diagram of a Loading-Jig Apparatus, as Part of a Laboratory Report

2. *Make a permanent record of your observations.* Keep a full record of your calculations, observations, and results in a special notebook. Don't ever write anything down on separate scraps of paper—not even your arithmetical

---

Experiment 3057 - October 27

Measurement of displacement, velocity and acceleration
EQUIPMENT: (a) Linear Variable Differential Transformer;
(b) an Oscilloscope; (c) an accelerometer; (d) an
Analyzer-Recorder; (e) a Vibrating Table.

– – – – – – – – – – – – – – – – – – –

Raw Data

FREQ(cps)	DISPLACEMENT	VELOCITY	ACCELERATION
40	Micro (mm) 1.6176 } Δ=101.9 mils 1.358 VIB. MTR. 97 mils	VIB. MTR. 29.2 $\frac{in}{sec}$	V.M. 9300 (in/sec²)
30	Micro (mm) 1.621 } Δ = 96.8 mils 1.375 VIB. MTR. 98 mils	VIB. MTR. 21.9 $\frac{in}{sec}$	V.M. 5700 (in/sec²)
20	Micro (mm) 1.609 } Δ = 94.7 mils 1.369	VIB. MTR. 14.9 $\frac{in}{sec}$	V.M. 2950 (in/sec²)
10	Micro (mm) 1.607 } Δ = 96.3 mils 1.363 VIB. MTR. 102 mils	VIB. MTR. 6.9 $\frac{in}{sec}$	V.M. 1020 (in/sec²)

FIGURE B.3 A Page from a Record Book, Showing Raw Data Gathered Directly from Measurements Made by Instruments

calculations. If you make mistakes, cross them out and go on from there, but keep everything as part of your complete record. Start your record of each experiment or laboratory session on a new page, headed with the date. This will give you a permanent log of all your data and your thinking for every problem on which you have worked—the raw materials for your final report.

3. *Organize the recorded data.* Arrange the data so that they will be clear and fully labeled for later reference. The few extra minutes you spend to make neat and orderly records during the lab period will save you time that might otherwise have to be spent deciphering sloppy notes (see Figure B.3).

4. *Do not trust yourself or the apparatus too much.* It is unwise to record a lot of untested numbers, dismantle the apparatus, and leave the laboratory before knowing whether your data are of any use. It is much better to do at least an approximate analysis (including rough graphs) of the data while they are being taken. Such a check will give you a chance to detect anything that is going wrong in time to do something about it—such as readjusting the apparatus, checking or repeating an observation, or asking your instructor for assistance.

5. *Baby the apparatus.* Poor performance in a laboratory is often due to carelessness, but it may also be the result of an uncooperative attitude. Don't be too ready to say the apparatus doesn't work or to believe it is limited in capability. Treat the apparatus tenderly, and coax out of it all the accuracy it can produce. Make note of its limitations, and watch it like a hawk for signs of strange behavior. No real equipment is quite like the ideal version pictured in a textbook or laboratory manual; each piece of apparatus has an individual "personality."

6. *Keep the purpose of the experiment in mind.* This can save you much wasted effort and keep you from overlooking the main point of the lab work.

7. *Write up your reports clearly, legibly, and concisely, in the proper form.* The writing style should be impersonal; in technical reports it is customary to use the passive voice (see Figure B.4). A laboratory report usually contains some or all of the following items:

Purpose (object): A statement explaining what the problem is

Theory: The background for the problem and the justification for your method of attack

Apparatus (equipment, materials): A listing and brief description of the essential apparatus, often including a sketch of the apparatus

Procedure: A step-by-step report of what you did

Results: A step-by-step record of your observations

Experiment 34

A.   PURPOSE: To observe the increase in birefringence of
nylon by increasing the orientation of fibers through
stretching, despite the thinning of the nylon by necking.

B.   PROCEDURE
     (a) A narrow strip of thin transparent nylon sheet,
     stretched in some spots and not stretched in others,
     was observed between crossed polarizers with low
     magnification.
     (b)About 1 mm diameter as-extruded nylon monofila-
     ment was stretched and the necking observed.
     (c) Textile-grade nylon fiber was observed as-
     extruded and stretched. The diameters and polariza-
     tion colors of each region of the fiber were noted.

C.   RESULTS
     (a)

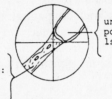

                                          unstretched nylon;
                                          polarization colors:
                                          1st order white.

stretched nylon;
polarization colors:
3rd order red and
green.

     (b) Nylon monofilament necked abruptly, rather than
     breaking, when pulled:

     (c) 16 mm objective, 1 eyepiece micrometer division =
     16.0 μ

	Diameter	Converted diameter	Retardation
Unstretched	4.3 div.	68.8 μ	200 μ
Stretched	1.9 div.	30.4 μ	1850 μ

	Birefringence
Unstretched	0.003
Stretched	0.059

D.   CONCLUSIONS
     Unstretched nylon fiber exhibited a 1st order white
     polarization color, i.e., showed very low bire-
     fringence. The birefringence was calculated to be
     about 0.003.
     When pulled in tension, the nylon fiber necked
     abruptly. The stretched portion of the sample showed
     3rd order and higher polarization colors, despite
     decreased thickness. This was due to a marked increase
     in birefringence, to about 0.059, resulting from the
     parallel orientation of fibers effected by stretching.
     Without polarizers, the nylon fiber appeared
     slightly greyed or opaqued where stretched. Orienting
     the polymer fibers leads to a decrease in clarity. Also,
     the stretching results in mechanical discontinuities
     which would tend to scatter the light.

FIGURE B.4 Sample Lab Report

Conclusion: A summary of your findings and an assessment of their accuracy, showing how your results succeed or fail in resolving the problem

Above all, in writing a report, remember that your purpose is to make your findings understandable to a reader. Make full use of your writing skills.

SUMMARY

How is learning science different from learning other subjects?

There are two differences. First, the terms, facts, and principles must be learned precisely. Second, the facts and problems are quantitative in nature.

What is meant by learning in clusters?

Learning in clusters is a matter of finding the relations among various pieces of information and then grouping the information in your mind according to those relations. It makes remembering much easier.

How can I improve my note taking in science lectures?

Concentrate on the ideas that are being presented, rather than on the words themselves. Use the Cornell System, which allows you to take, review, recite, and consolidate your notes more easily. Convert your notes into master summary sheets.

What's the best time to ask a question in class?

The best time is at the beginning of the lecture. The instructor may make use of your question during the lecture.

What's the best way to solve a test problem?

The best way is to remember how you solved a similar problem before and to do the same things again. Recall requires experience, and the only way you can get experience is with plenty of practice. Work out all the assigned problems, and then look for some more to work on.

How should I handle a type of problem that I've never faced before?

Be logical and systematic. First, figure out just what you need to find. Then try to plot a logical course from the given quantities to the unknown quantities, or vice versa. Once you

	have plotted this course, convert the steps into equations and solve them.
What's the key to answering discussion questions?	Figure out what sort of answer each question requires. Then try to connect the question with your clusters of learned facts and principles. Once you've made the connection, write out your answer in clear, precise language.
What is the objective of the seven hints for doing lab work?	The objective is to make sure you have all the information or data you need, in a logical and legible form, to communicate your lab results clearly and precisely.

HAVE YOU MISSED SOMETHING?

Sentence Completion

Complete the following sentences with one of the three words or phrases listed below each sentence.

1. The reason for the insistence on precision is that the sciences deal with _____ .
   creative ideas   measurable things   the frontiers of knowledge

2. Science textbooks are packed with information, so read them
   _____ .
   for scientific principles   sentence by sentence   for major ideas

3. In working on experiments in the laboratory, its is important to record _____ .
   only the major findings   only the steps leading toward proving a principle   even the minutest steps

Matching

In each blank space in the left column, write the letter preceding the phrase in the right column that matches the left item best.

_____	**1.** Clustering	a. Is used for scientific measurement
_____	**2.** Precision	b. Realized that people mentally visualize abstract concepts
_____	**3.** Questioning	c. Is characteristic of the sciences.
_____	**4.** Metric system	d. Are needed to do good lab reports
		e. Helps to fill gaps in understanding
_____	**5.** Writing skills	f. Involves placing facts and ideas into groups and categories
_____	**6.** Maxwell	

True-False

Write *T* beside the *true* statements and *F* beside the *false* statements.

_____ **1.** Complex problems are often made up of simple parts.

_____ **2.** No real practice is needed to answer a discussion question.

_____ **3.** A science should be studied as if it were made up of isolated facts.

_____ **4.** A quantitative principle is one that is stated in mathematical terms.

_____ **5.** Your lab equipment is always right and should be trusted.

Multiple Choice

Choose the phrase that completes each of the following sentences most accurately, and circle the letter that precedes it.

1. The secret of solving science problems is
    a. practice.
    b. genius.
    c. questioning.
    d. creativity.

2. Your science lecture notes should focus less on words and more on
   a. specific data.
   b. facts.
   c. ideas.
   d. formulas.

3. Science is different from many other subjects in that most of the ideas
   are stated
   a. quantitatively.
   b. repeatedly.
   c. obscurely.
   d. qualitatively.

4. Much of science deals with explaining
   a. isolated facts.
   b. weights and measures.
   c. relationships.
   d. controversial theories.

5. New terms in a science course should be
   a. simplified, if possible.
   b. mastered, as with any new words.
   c. taken only from lectures, not readings.
   d. kept in a separate vocabulary notebook.

6. The most successful way to solve a problem is to
   a. ask the instructor a precise, well-thought-out question.
   b. use a programmed workbook or other study guide.
   c. write down everything you think may be pertinent.
   d. recall how you solved a similar problem.

Short Answer

Supply a brief answer for each of the following items.

1. Single out a particular science and explain how its orientation and
   emphases differ from those of other sciences.

2. When and how should you ask questions in a science course?

3. In answering discussion questions, where do the difficulties normally
   appear?

4. How should you use a laboratory apparatus?

Vocabulary Building

Directions: Make a light check mark (✓) alongside one of the three words (choices) that most nearly expresses the meaning of the italicized word in the phrases that are in the left-hand column. (Answers are given on page 119.)

	1	2	3
1. extreme *precision*	randomness	accuracy	anticipation
2. can be *intimidating*	suggestive	reassuring	frightening
3. precise *terminology*	nomenclature	finality	insect study
4. in *manipulating*	handling	scattering	confirming
5. write *concisely*	descriptively	succinctly	rationally
6. appeared *opaque*	translucent	transparent	nontransparent
7. have been *stymied*	blocked	organized	enlightened
8. to *wrest* control	seize	give	ruin
9. number of *allegations*	denials	parables	declarations
10. *predatory* behavior	predictable	compassionate	rapacious
11. increase its *scrutiny*	examination	disregard	usefulness
12. his *diminutive* sidekick	unintelligent	enormous	undersized
13. a powerful *taboo*	prohibition	endorsement	enchantment
14. weigh the *credibility*	dubiousness	plausibility	unreasonableness
15. its *ultimate* goal	private	first	final
16. *acrimonious* argument	bitter	lively	friendly
17. *diametrically* opposed	logically	circuitously	exactly oppositely
18. an *opportunistic* suitor	wealthy	unlucky	taking advantage
19. *unsolicited* offer	unasked for	sought after	unthoughtful
20. a *candid* memorandum	diplomatic	truthful	surprizing
21. *lucrative* for dealers	ridiculous	marginal	profitable
22. investors were *unfazed*	unabashed	disconcerted	upset
23. to *revoke* articles	withdraw	restore	maintain
24. *optimistic* assessment	largest	pessimistic	confident
25. expressed *skepticism*	disbelief	certainty	confidence

Additional Multiple-Choice Questions

1. Science is a brazen challenge against the
   a. understood.
   b. unknown.
   c. unequaled.
   d. undone.

2. A student with a positive critical attitude expects to be
    a. famous.
    b. correct.
    c. challenged.
    d. convinced.

3. Science problems are primarily
    a. imitative.
    b. qualitative.
    c. annotative.
    d. quantitative.

4. In science vocabulary, unlike most other vocabulary, you can't rely on
    a. meaning.
    b. spelling.
    c. context.
    d. grammar.

5. *Chunking* is simply the process of placing ideas and facts into
    a. sentences.
    b. context.
    c. categories.
    d. images.

6. Complex problems are usually composed of
    a. simple parts.
    b. complex rules.
    c. several factors.
    d. simple addition.

7. You can check a problem by estimating the answer's
    a. variable.
    b. quotient.
    c. magnitude.
    d. amplitude.

8. In a discussion question the trick is to comprehend the author's
    a. resources.
    b. materials.
    c. outline.
    d. purpose.

9. In the laboratory you should learn to trust your
    a. results.
    b. diagrams.
    c. memory.
    d. partner.

10. In writing a report, your main purpose is to make the findings
    a. variable.
    b. plausible.
    c. understandable.
    d. recoverable.

ANSWERS FOR STUDYING SCIENCE

Sentence Completion

1. measurable things   2. sentence by sentence   3. even the minutest steps

Matching

1. f   2. c   3. e   4. a   5. d   6. b

True-False

1. T   2. F   3. F   4. T   5. F

Multiple Choice

1. a   2. c   3. a   4. c   5. b   6. d

Vocabulary Building

1. 2   2. 3   3. 1   4. 1   5. 2   6. 3   7. 1   8. 1   9. 3   10. 3   11. 1   12. 3   13. 1
14. 2   15. 3   16. 1   17. 3   18. 3   19. 1   20. 2   21. 3   22. 1   23. 1   24. 3
25. 1

Additional Multiple-Choice Questions

1. b   2. d   3. d   4. c   5. c   6. a   7. c   8. d   9. c   10. c

The sum of human wisdom is not contained in any one language, and no single language is CAPABLE of expressing all forms and degrees of human comprehension.

EZRA POUND

(1885–1972), poet, critic, translator, and editor

C

Supplementary Chapter C

STUDYING FOREIGN LANGUAGES

Knowing a foreign language gives you direct access to great thoughts, experiences, and cultures that would otherwise be out of reach. Getting someone to translate something for you, reading translations of literature, or watching a foreign film dubbed into English or with English subtitles is like shadowboxing. It is no way to get the full benefit of the experience. This chapter discusses

- Learning to listen and speak in a foreign language

- Learning to read and write in a foreign language

- Getting the most from your textbook

- Getting the most out of class time

- Special notes on culture

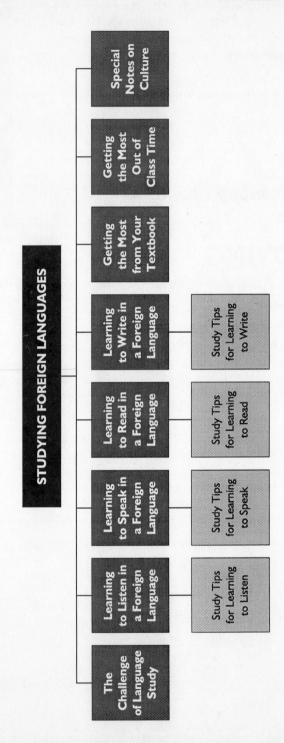

If you find language courses easy, you may have a special, natural talent, or you may have greater motivation and enthusiasm than many. Even for you, however, learning a foreign language requires a lot of hard work.

THE CHALLENGE OF LANGUAGE STUDY

Language study is different from most other disciplines in that it entails learning both facts and skills. In addition to learning "facts" such as grammar rules and vocabulary, you must learn how to use those "facts" for listening, speaking, reading, and writing. There is a lot of overlap among these skills, but being good at one does not necessarily mean being good at the others (virtually no one is equally good at them all). Knowing this should help you understand why your language study goes better at some times than it does at others. Identifying the skills you are best at and determining how you learn best will go a long way toward helping you use your study time effectively.

Another peculiarity of language study is that learning to use a language well is partly a matter of habit—this is especially true of speaking. You speak your native language fluently, but you don't do so by thinking *about* the language. You didn't even learn it in the first place by "thinking." Instead, you listened to other people and imitated what they said. By doing this repeatedly, you eventually developed the habits that allow you to speak with ease. You think not about *how* to use the language but, rather, about *what* you are going to say. If your native language is English, for instance, you don't stop to think about saying "he works" (with an *-s* ending) and "they work" (with no *-s* ending). Nor do you have to stop to think about pronouncing the word *the* as "thee" in front of words that begin with a vowel ("the apple, the orange") but as "thuh" in front of words that begin with a consonant ("the peach, the banana"). You do things like that as matters of habit.

To learn any language, you have to repeat a lot of what you learn again and again until it becomes second nature to you. When you were learning your native language, you had essentially full-time practice without making any effort. But when you try to learn a foreign language, you are handicapped in a couple of ways. First, you are unlikely to have enough time for practice. Second, you already have a set of language habits that will interfere with the new habits you are trying to develop. Don't be surprised if your brain has trouble coping at first. It is quite normal for people learning a new language to get their language habits a bit mixed up.

If learning a new language seems beyond you, remind yourself that every so-called foreign language is native to some people. Granted, the native learner had some advantages that you don't have when you approach a language as a second or other language. The chief advantage is age: It is easiest to learn a language when you are very young. The critical thing to keep in mind, however, is that the language can be and is learned by lots of people—most of them no smarter than you.

Most of us take years to learn our own language well, to use it with a reasonable amount of sophistication. At that rate, we're left with relatively little time to go through the process again, with another language. Besides, by the time you are in school, you are already past the "ideal" age for language learning, so it's too late to learn a new language in quite the way you learned your first. But don't worry, because there is another way to proceed.

You can use the rational skills that you didn't possess as a child to help learn a foreign language. When you were a child, you wouldn't have been able to cope with grammar rules at all. But now you can understand how the new language is put together, how it works, and how it differs from your native language. That information can speed up the learning process considerably.

Keep in mind, though, that learning grammar is not an end in itself. Rather, it is a way to make the imitation part of learning language more successful. If you understand the grammar as an adult and practice repeating and imitating as an uninhibited child would, you'll be able to overcome some of the disadvantages of not being a native learner.

LEARNING TO LISTEN IN A FOREIGN LANGUAGE

Although speaking might seem to be the most interesting and important skill to learn in another language, proper listening really has to come first. Don't confuse listening with hearing (this distinction is discussed in Chapter 9). You are likely to understand what you hear only when you have learned to listen.

When we hear people speaking a language we do not know, most of us think they are talking impossibly fast. Studies of recorded speech have shown, however, that speakers of most languages tend to utter very nearly the same number of syllables per minute when they speak at a normal rate. What makes them difficult to understand is not the speed of their speech but, rather, our not knowing where the syllables (or even the words) break. Everything seems to run together into a torrent of sound.

Listening is really a matter of learning to discriminate sounds. In English, for instance, it matters a lot whether there is a *d* or a *t* sound at the end of a word. The word *had* is not at all the same as *hat*, and you need to listen closely to hear the difference so that you know which word is meant. When the language is unfamiliar, you have to pay extra close attention.

English has a lot of word pairs that won't seem similar to you at all, because you know the language, but that could easily be confusing to someone trying to learn the language. Think about *pin* and *pan, tin* and *thin, sin* and *fin, sheet* and *shoot, but* and *putt.* The trick in learning a new language is to train yourself to listen carefully to new sounds and sound combinations— and to new words. You need to concentrate especially hard in the beginning so that you can distinguish sounds, syllables, words, and intonation patterns that may turn out to be important in the new language.

Study Tips for Learning to Listen

Rule number one for learning to listen effectively is: Concentrate! Casual listening will result in mere hearing. Rule number two is: Do your listening practice in small doses. In other words, limit the amount of time you engage in strict listening practice at any one sitting, and limit the amount you try to accomplish at any one sitting.

If you concentrate too hard on listening well, you'll probably grow tired. So give yourself a break by not overdoing it. Fifteen minutes of intensive listening work in a language lab—even when the practice includes repeating as well as listening—is enough for most people. (Thirty minutes of casual listening isn't nearly so helpful.) Going to the lab twice a day for fifteen minutes each time may not be efficient or even possible in your schedule, though. If that's the case, go for a half hour, but at the end of each ten or fifteen minutes stand up and touch your toes three times or do something else to allow your brain to relax for a moment.

Try to concentrate on a small task. If you find it difficult at first to make sense of the sounds and sound combinations in the new language, try breaking the task down. Instead of listening to a sentence with the aim of understanding the whole thing the first time through, listen just for a particular sound or a particular word. (How many times does it occur?) Then listen again, trying to pick up additional sounds or words.

Of course, in real life you can't play back a tape to listen to a sentence numerous times (though you can—and should—learn how to ask a conversational partner to repeat what he or she has said or to speak more slowly). But at the practice stage, it is both fair and sensible to play things back. Remember, you are trying initially to break down that torrent of sound into discrete elements that make sense to you.

Another strategy is to listen for the gist of what is being said—whether in a sentence, a dialogue, a paragraph, or a story. Even in your native language, you don't necessarily understand (or even hear) every single word. So why hold yourself to such an impossibly high standard in a new language? Eventually, you'll want to get to the point where you can and do get almost every word on the first pass, just as you do in your native language. At first, however, it's excellent practice to see whether you can at least get the drift of what is being said. This is called *global understanding,* meaning that you have a general (not a specific or local) idea of the topic even if you miss most of the details. Learning to get the drift is a critical part of listening comprehension. And, in any case, it's a good idea not to try to do too much at once.

Here's how to do it. Listen for familiar words. Try to pick out nouns and verbs. Learn to filter out the little words like articles and conjunctions at first; even adjectives and adverbs are usually unimportant when you are after global understanding. But listen carefully for powerful little words like *not,* which can significantly alter the meaning. Jot down words and ideas as you catch them (make your notes in the language you are studying). Then go back and listen again. Confirm what you heard by checking what you are listening to against what you jotted down. Try to fill in a few gaps.

For instance, on the first pass you may have understood that John did something, but you may not be sure what he did to whom or when or why. Before listening a second time, decide what additional information you would most like to have, which of your mental question marks it would be most helpful to eliminate. Then listen for that one thing. (What John did is likely to be more important than anything else.) It's possible that the information you are listening for is not in the passage. If you don't get it after a couple of tries, listen for something else. Go back and listen as many times as you need to, until you get all your questions answered.

When you are pretty sure that you understand the whole passage, put your notes aside and listen one more time. Try to let the rhythm and the sounds convey their message to you directly without thinking about the content in English. This is your chance to consolidate your learning. (The principle of consolidation is discussed in Chapter 5.)

LEARNING TO SPEAK IN A FOREIGN LANGUAGE

Because speaking is the most common, everyday way to communicate with language, it is probably the most useful of the language skills. If you can speak the language, you will almost certainly be able to read it, and you will have a solid base for writing as well.

The listening skill is crucial to learning to speak. Listening practice not only helps you understand others but also provides models for you to imitate in your own speaking.

Remember that language is a set of habits. Grammar rules explain some aspects of the way the language works, but thinking about those rules is not very helpful when you are trying to speak the language. The only way to learn the language is to learn the habits (through repetition and lots of practice), not to think about them. Instead of organizing, analyzing, and interpreting factual data, you must practice the material you've heard in class again and again until it becomes second nature. That means memorizing.

Children learn languages by imitating first the short phrases and expressions they hear frequently and need most. Those are the kinds of things you will learn first in your new language as well. The more complicated and abstract ideas that you are accustomed to being able to express in your native language are likely to be harder; you mustn't expect to be able to talk at the same level in the new language right away. You may feel you've been reduced to the intellectual level of a ten-year-old for a while. But memorizing carefully what is modeled for you, and resisting the temptation to say things you haven't yet heard, will pay off. You'll end up making fewer mistakes, and you'll establish good foundations for your later language development.

One reason it is so important to limit yourself to the vocabulary and structures that have been modeled for you is that languages do not all work in the same way. Words that look and sometimes even sound alike in two languages do not necessarily mean the same thing. Also, every language has idiomatic expressions that cannot be constructed on the basis of rules.

An *idiom* is an expression with a peculiar, individual cast. It may mean something other than what the sum of its parts seems to imply. "It's raining cats and dogs" has nothing to do with animals, for instance, as every native speaker of English knows. Or an idiom may be the customary way of saying something. You could say "Happy Christmas" and "Merry Birthday," but you don't. The same ideas are frequently conveyed differently in any pair of languages. You and your friends would say in English, "We are hungry and thirsty." In many other languages, people say, "We have hunger and thirst."

You cannot know idioms ahead of time, and you cannot expect to figure them out. You have to hear the idiom models and imitate them so often that you stop thinking about whether they are different from what you would say in your native language. Idioms have to become second nature through memorization.

Study Tips for Learning to Speak

One of the advantages children have in learning languages is that they tend to be amused by imitating new sounds. Adults, unfortunately, are likely to feel embarrassed by their attempts to say things in a new way. So rule number one in learning to speak a foreign language is: Throw caution to the wind! Try to get a kick out of the new sounds. Use exaggerated facial expressions—use those muscles!—to practice what you are saying. The odds are that the stranger you sound to yourself at first, the closer you are to imitating the new sounds correctly.

Rule number two is: Do all your practicing out loud. Some people even say the louder the better—if you are going to make a mistake, make it boldly! Reading material silently is fine if you are simply trying to understand the content. In doing that, however, you are learning only how the language is symbolized on paper, which doesn't have much to do with speaking. If you are going to develop new oral habits, you need oral practice. (Review the benefits of recitation discussed in Chapter 5.)

There is another reason for practicing out loud. When you read silently, you are using only your visual memory. But if you study out loud, you double your efficiency by adding auditory memory. You remember things you have heard *and* seen better than those you have merely seen. Beyond that, saying things out loud means you are adding motor memory, which generally quadruples efficiency. Motor memory is the memory of what you do with your muscles. One indication of its efficiency is that nobody ever forgets how to ride a bicycle.

Another way to put motor memory to work for you is to write out what you are trying to memorize. Read a passage (a sentence, a phrase, a word) out loud; then copy it, saying it again while you write. Now you've got eyes, ears, tongue, and hands all helping your brain. A side benefit of doing oral work this way is that so much of you is involved that you have to concentrate intensively.

Still another parallel exists between learning to listen and learning to speak, and that is the importance of not trying to take on too much at once. Most children are pretty good at memorizing. Adults, however, seem to be much less efficient. It's not that they can't memorize, just that they have to work at it. The first crucial step in this work is to break material to be memorized into small units.

What counts as small? Some people seem to be able to memorize whole paragraphs easily. Most, however, find even a sentence too much if it is really new. They need to break sentences into phrases. And if they are tired or if the passage is especially difficult, they may need to tackle smaller units than usual. How small depends in part on individuals' learning styles; there is no magic formula.

One trick that works well for most people is to tackle sentences backward. If you learn the end of a sentence first, you'll probably learn it best. Then when you've built up to saying the whole sentence, you'll always be working toward what you know instead of struggling toward something new. Try it with this sample in English: "I'm going to Paris next summer with my whole family."

Start by isolating meaningful phrases or word clusters. "I'm going / to Paris / next summer / with my whole family." (If the words are especially difficult to say, you could break a sentence like this into even smaller units.) Now practice the last phrase—"with my whole family"—over and over until you can say it easily, without thinking about it. Then practice saying "next summer" until that phrase slips smoothly off your tongue, before you put the two together: "next summer with my whole family." Then work on "to Paris," "to Paris next summer," and "to Paris next summer with my whole family." Now you are ready to work on the last phrase (actually the first one in the sentence): "I'm going." Finally, just build that into the rest of the sentence.

This procedure may sound arduous, but it takes less time to do than to explain. And it does work, if you are patient and systematic. You may want to reserve this technique for particularly long and complicated sentences; you probably won't need to do quite so much repetition with short ones.

Another aspect of breaking your memory work into small units has to do with the amount of time you spend at any one sitting. You should be able to work effectively on oral (speaking) work longer at one time than on aural (listening) exercises. One thing is virtually certain. If you spend two uninterrupted hours trying to memorize new material, you are unlikely to get the most out of your time.

How quickly any one person's powers of concentration diminish depends on lots of factors; you'll need to figure out for yourself how long your attention span is for different kinds of work, how much you can "take." Be honest! It won't help if you are too easy on yourself. You should be able to increase the amount of time you can concentrate as you get better at the language. For starters, try from twenty to thirty minutes at the most. Then do something else: Work on another subject, walk around the block, eat lunch, whatever. But then come back for another twenty- or thirty-minute stint. A couple of hours divided up in this way will produce better results than working straight through for two hours would.

Frequent small doses seem to work well for another reason, too. Learning a language is a cumulative process. Much of the new material you will be asked to learn as you go along—vocabulary and grammar as well as the conversational patterns you are memorizing—builds on what you have already learned. The new material either won't make sense or will be harder to learn if you have not mastered what went before or have forgotten it. Language teachers sometimes talk about "frequent reentry" of material, which means bringing things you have already learned back at frequent intervals. Most language textbooks are written in a way that tries to accomplish this, but you can help yourself by reviewing frequently and by doing assignments quickly, intensely, and more than once.

A final word must be said here about memory work, even though it has to do with aspects of language learning other than just the speaking skill. If you want to learn to speak a new language as an adult, you have to do more than merely imitate what others say. You also have to do lots of memorizing of vocabulary, the rules of grammar, and so on. Apply the principles and theories about forgetting discussed in Chapter 5. And break your work—lists

of words, for instance—into meaningful blocks. Organize words to be memorized in a way that makes sense to you, regardless of how they appear in your
textbook. Group them by gender, by subject matter, by parts of speech, by
length—whatever works for you.

Above all, try to fit the rules of grammar into a context as you work on
learning them. In this sense, you *do* need to think; memorizing is not sufficient
for the adult language learner. You will help yourself enormously if, as you
memorize, you think about the grammatical explanations that accompany
each bit of new material. The grammatical section of a new lesson may tell
you, for example, about verb endings. After you have read the section and
have spoken the examples out loud, start memorizing the new material. Every
time you say a verb form, fit it mentally into the scheme that has just been
explained to you.

LEARNING TO READ IN A FOREIGN LANGUAGE

When you read something in your native language, you do not necessarily
understand every word, and you certainly don't pronounce each word to
yourself. That is worth keeping in mind, because there is a tendency to think
you have to understand everything when you read a foreign language.
Instead, your goal should be to pick up a foreign language text (a book, a
newspaper, a brochure) or look at a sign (directions, instructions, advertisements) and understand what it is about just as you would a similar item in
your native language.

Just as you probably use different reading techniques in your native
language, depending on the type of material and the situation, you need to
develop different techniques for reading in a new language. First and fore-
most, this means thinking about the kind of material you are reading. Just
because they are all course assignments does not mean you should look at
them all in the same way. The precise meaning of each word is likely to matter
more in poetry than in a novel. A close analysis of details is more important
if you are going to discuss the relative merits of two proposals than if you are
merely reading the minutes of a meeting. And the directions for putting
something together need to be read differently from the words of a business
letter. Learning to read is not just one kind of activity.

Although reading in a foreign language has a lot in common with reading
in your own language, it presents some special challenges. The whole framework of what you are trying to read in another language may be foreign to
you, so it's likely to be hard for you to get started. The percentage of unfamiliar
words is likely to be uncomfortably high. These problems can be overcome,
however. Keep in mind that reading in a foreign language should ultimately

be like reading in your own language. It's a way to get information, to be exposed to new ideas, to pass the time pleasurably. These, not solving linguistic puzzles, are the legitimate goals for this activity.

One thing you will gradually discover is that reading is both easier and harder than listening and speaking. It is easier because when you read you can go back and reread, you can slow down or speed up, you can proceed at your own pace. Conversations don't work that way. On the other hand, when people take the trouble to write, they tend to express their ideas in a more complex way than they would have done in conversation. The ideas themselves may in fact be more complicated. This can make reading a challenge at times. Don't be surprised if you have to work hard at your foreign language reading, at least initially. Then again, the rewards of success are high. You will be moving steadily toward the point where you can vastly increase the range of information directly available to you.

Study Tips for Learning to Read

Because the single biggest hurdle in foreign language reading is usually the unfamiliar vocabulary, it merits special attention. Rule number one for learning to read in a foreign language is: Make sure you don't confuse *translating* with *reading*.

The whole point of learning to read a foreign language is to avoid having to translate. Worrying about the exact meaning of each word and phrase you come to in a foreign language text is really undercutting the point of what you are doing. Your aim should be to *learn to think in the new language*, at least well enough to understand what you are reading without translating it. To achieve this, you need to have memorized standard expressions, you need to have developed a good grasp of the grammar, and you have to be constantly expanding your vocabulary.

Most foreign language courses do not require you to read things that really are too hard for you. What you read at first will often be made up mostly of words you have already heard and learned to say; indeed, you should get a nice "Aha!" sense of recognition from reading them. At the very least, reading selections are likely to be on topics you have already been exposed to, so the context and some of the vocabulary will be familiar.

As a result, some of the listening techniques previously discussed can be applied to learning to read as well. You don't have to and shouldn't try to get everything at once. Expect to go over your reading assignments several times. Three quick readings, done systematically, are almost always better than one plodding one. Also remember what was said in Chapter 5 about study techniques for memory work and about massed and distributed practice.

Even before you start, check to see whether there are questions at the end of the passage you are working on. Studying the questions before you read can help set the stage, give you a context, and tell you what to read for. On your first pass, then, you might try to get the gist of the selection. (In a difficult assignment, too, you may want to tackle just one paragraph at a time.)

You should make this first pass without looking up any words, even if the passage contains a lot you do not know. Remember, you're just trying to get a general feel for what is under discussion, to get global understanding. Once you have done that, perhaps making notes for yourself of key words to help fix the basic topic in your mind, you're ready to begin a different, more precise kind of reading. But even then you should resist the temptation to check the meaning of each word.

Rule number two for reading in a foreign language is: Learn to make intelligent guesses. If you are going to learn how to read for content and pleasure, you need to be able to figure out what a word means from the context in which it is used. You do this all the time in your native language; you read and understand a lot of words you never use in speaking or writing.

To deduce the meanings of words from their contexts—or to remember the meanings of words you have looked up—read them more than once. As a rule of thumb, don't look up a word until you have encountered it three times without being able to figure it out. This will save you a lot of time. You are also more likely to remember a word you've figured out from context than one you've looked up, especially if you looked up a great many words during that one reading session.

Sometimes it is not clear how far you have to read to get the context of something. Perhaps the best way to proceed is to read through the first sentence and then keep on reading until you get lost. You may be able to follow along for a paragraph, a page, or even a whole assignment. Once you begin to get lost, stop and go back to the beginning. Read along again until you come to the first word you still don't know. Underline the word so you can find it again quickly. Continue in this fashion to the point where you left off the first time, and then start over once more. If, on the third reading, you still cannot guess the meaning of a word you have underlined, look it up. Put a dot in the margin of the vocabulary or dictionary page beside the word to show you had to look it up. (Later, if you have to look the same word up again, add a dot. This will help you keep track of words that give you extra trouble, so you can isolate and study them.) Find the English translation that best fits your sentence. Then, turning back to the text, reread the phrase in which the word occurs, trying to fix its meaning in your mind as you do so. Go through the entire first passage this way, looking up only the words you absolutely have to and making intelligent guesses at the others. Then tackle the next section in the same manner, until you have read about half of your assignment.

At that point, take a short break. Then reread the part you have already finished before you go on. Rereading while the section you have worked on is still fresh in your memory will really tie down the loose ends. If you wait until later on, much of it will have grown cold. Besides, seeing how easily you can read what you have worked so hard on should motivate you to proceed with the second half of your assignment. Go through it in the same way, looking up only the words you cannot guess. When you've taken the second short break and reread the second half of your assignment, read quickly through the whole thing. Consolidate what you've learned.

If you come to words, idioms, or grammatical constructions you cannot sort out, underline them. If after your second or third honest try you still cannot figure them out, put a vertical line in the margin to remind you to ask your instructor for an explanation. If you have been thorough about applying everything you know and systematic about making intelligent guesses, you will probably discover that you are not the only one in class who had difficulty with those spots.

LEARNING TO WRITE IN A FOREIGN LANGUAGE

Of the four language skills under discussion here, writing—at least writing on a sophisticated, adult level—is probably the most difficult. When you consider how hard it is for most people to write stylishly and clearly even in their native language, this is not surprising. Thus no one will expect you to produce very long or complicated written assignments early in your language study.

Nonetheless, the ability to put ideas into writing is an important part of mastering another language. Learning to be accurate in the production of language as it is symbolized on paper is part of any foreign language course. Writing is a legitimate end in itself; it also involves motor memory, and it helps consolidate all aspects of what you are learning in the language.

The simplest aspect of writing is producing individual words and phrases on paper correctly. And essential to that is mastering the language's sound-symbol correspondence. In other words, you have to learn to spell words, not just to recognize them. In fact, early assignments may include having you copy words, sentences, or dialogues from your textbook. Carrying out such simple tasks is one way to get started on good writing habits. Accurately copying sentences that are known to be correct models keeps you from making mistakes. Writing entails much more than putting words on paper, however. Even before you advance to lengthy, creative, or scholarly writing, some tips may be useful.

Study Tips for Learning to Write

Just as learning to speak correctly means learning to listen carefully to models and imitating them, learning to write correctly requires learning to observe written models closely enough to imitate them. Rule number one for writing is: Make sure you learn the spelling, gender, and declension (or conjugation) of each new word as it comes along. Just looking at a new word, or even saying it out loud, is not sufficient. Spell it out loud. Copy it out (think again about using 3 × 5 cards), spelling it aloud again as you write it.

The same applies to whole phrases, sentences, and paragraphs. Good oral and aural habits can help you in writing, just as writing can help your oral performance. Early assignments will almost certainly require you to put together, in a sensible sequence, sentences you already have read and know how to say. Take advantage of the existing models in your textbook to make sure you are reproducing such bits of language accurately when you write them.

Another useful suggestion was made in connection with learning to speak: Try to resist the temptation—at first—to express thoughts as complicated as those you are accustomed to writing in your native language. Build a solid base by getting the simple things right, often; the more complex matters will begin to fall into place later.

Rule number two for writing—especially as you move toward creating original sentences and paragraphs—is: Follow the same procedures and steps you would for a written assignment in your native language. Although the requirements with respect to length and complexity of topic will be very different, the basic concerns are the same: Define your topic precisely; organize your thoughts carefully; and make notes or an outline before you start to do the actual writing. You should follow these steps even for a very short assignment.

Above all, allow time to edit what you have written. If editing is an important part of writing in your native language, consider how much more important it will be in a language that is relatively new to you! Leave yourself time for a break between the initial writing and the editing (a day or more is ideal) so that you can look at what you have written with fresh eyes.

Remember, too, that editing is a complicated job. You should not expect to do an adequate job of editing simply by rereading what you have written. You'll need to go through your finished draft once to check mechanical details like spelling and punctuation. Then you'll need to go through again to check the grammar and at least once more to make sure the ideas you want to express are coming across clearly and correctly. Nothing less will do. This process sounds time consuming, and it is. But it is also much more efficient than trying to tackle everything at once, and more reliable than skipping one or another of these steps. If you break the task into its separate parts, you can be reasonably sure that the time you spend will be used effectively.

You should read your paper out loud to test the sound. If you have been doing most of your homework orally, as has been recommended, you will gradually develop an ear for how the language ought to sound. Does your writing flow smoothly? Are the sentences too long and therefore hard to read? Are they too short and therefore choppy? Is it easy to follow your point? Even better than just reading your work to yourself is to get a classmate to listen, to serve as a friendly critic. Offer to do the same for her or him. The practice of reading, listening, and criticizing will help both of you.

Finally, type or write a clean copy of your paper to turn in. You do not want the evidence of your hard work to get lost in a sloppy presentation. Allow yourself plenty of time for this step, and consider it one last chance to make changes or corrections, if the need arises.

Writing well *is* hard work. Don't let the difficulty of the process surprise or discourage you. By following the models in your textbook, you are bound to do more right than wrong. You will get better as you go along, if you proceed cautiously.

GETTING THE MOST FROM YOUR TEXTBOOK

Surveying your foreign language textbook is especially important. Language teachers are constantly developing new methods to help students learn foreign languages efficiently and thoroughly, and their efforts are reflected in the textbooks. But because language learning is such a complex matter, the books differ; no one book can possibly be the best in every regard for every student. You need to become familiar with *your* book so that you can make it mesh with your learning style.

For example, some books give grammar explanations and rules first and then provide exercises for you to do. Others provide models for you to follow in doing the exercises, giving you a chance to figure out the rules before you read any explanations of them. This is the difference, roughly, between a deductive and an inductive approach, from the student's point of view. Each method has much to be said in its favor. What you need to do is be sure you understand which one your book is using; only then will you be able to work effectively with it.

If your book gives rules and explanations first (and encourages you to work deductively), you don't necessarily have to do every assignment in that way. You may discover that you learn better by doing the exercises first and trying to establish the rules on the basis of what you are doing (you may work better inductively) and then checking what you have figured out against what the book tells you. Most foreign language textbooks are deliberately written so that they can be used in a variety of ways. Feel free to experiment a bit until you determine how your book works best for you.

Once you have become familiar with your book and have made any necessary adjustments in the way you approach assignments to fit your learning style, stick with your system. Developing a systematic approach to your language study is an important part of building new language habits.

Whatever system you develop, it should not entail shortcuts. The authors of foreign language textbooks include every exercise, explanation, and example for a reason. Furthermore, if a workbook or a lab manual and recorded materials accompany your textbook, be faithful about using them as well. Remember, learning a language is a complex task that is best done in frequent small doses. The various components of your foreign language program are designed to help strengthen the habits you are building.

One of the best ways to build good habits is to do exercises more than once. The second time will not take so long as the first, and you will have more than doubled the odds of retaining what you've learned. Doing an exercise is one thing; learning the material well enough to retain it is quite different. Making a new language second nature requires extra effort.

To prevent the repetition of exercises from being boring, adapt the exercises slightly the second time through. If the exercise is oral, write it out the second time. If it is written, say it out loud. Start at the end of an exercise and work backward the second time. Combine related exercises in your textbook and your workbook. And so on. Try to think of ways to put every kind of memory (visual, oral, auditory, motor) to work. With a little creative effort and extra time, you can make your textbook do double duty for you.

In addition, follow the suggestions in Chapter 11 about marking your book and using the margins to ask yourself questions. Put vertical lines or dots in the margins to remind yourself of trouble spots. Figure out other ways to make the book yours. Make it help you learn so that eventually you can become independent of it.

Resist the temptation to write interlinear translations in your foreign language textbook. Such translations guarantee that you won't learn to think in the other language, because your eyes will keep drifting to the words you have written in. Translations also prevent you from getting valuable additional practice with the foreign language material by going through it a second time or in class—again, because your eyes will travel to the translations instead of to the original text.

GETTING THE MOST OUT OF CLASS TIME

Any time you emerge from a foreign language class without being tired, you probably haven't been working hard enough. Your few hours of classes each week are a substitute for the countless hours you had for listening and imitating when you were learning your native language. You have to concentrate hard during those few hours; the effort of concentration *should* make you tired, even if you are enjoying the class.

If your instructor has decorated the classroom with pictures and artifacts from the country whose language you are studying, take full advantage of this atmosphere, where it will seem appropriate to speak a language other than English. You should do everything you can to add to and maintain the illusion that you are in a foreign language environment, because your hours in class are the closest you will come to it in most foreign language courses. Learn to greet your classmates and instructor in the new language. This will help set the mood and save you from switching back and forth between English and your new language—a sure way to interrupt the process of establishing new language habits.

Thus, even when your textbook presents material in English, try to raise questions and ask for clarifications in the foreign language. Try to think in your new language. It will help a lot if you seek out others in your class willing to make the same effort. Sit next to them, and arrange study sessions with them.

Because of the cumulative nature of language learning, falling behind is a more serious problem than in other courses. Catching up is extremely difficult, so be very disciplined about doing all your assignments completely and on time. If you have trouble, get help right away. There are several ways to get help. You can go over things again (after taking a break to clear your head). You can ask a classmate who is doing well to help you. You can go to your instructor. And if you know someone who has a different textbook for the same language, you may occasionally want to see how that text presents the subject that is giving you difficulty. The different or additional explanation may do the trick for you.

Getting the most out of class is closely related to getting the most out of your textbook. The primary watchwords for making class time worthwhile are: Prepare before class. Attend every class. Work hard in class.

SPECIAL NOTES ON CULTURE

The skills discussed in this chapter do not tell the whole story when it comes to learning a foreign language. One reason for studying a different language is to learn about native speakers of the language you are studying—the places they live and the lives they lead. You are trying to gain access to a culture. Learning a language and learning a culture—by which we generally mean both high culture (art, history, music, literature) and aspects of everyday living (people's customs, habits, likes and dislikes, food, clothing)—are integrally related. Those cultural matters are to a considerable extent the subject matter of foreign language courses, though it is easy to lose sight of them when you are deeply involved in learning vocabulary and grammar. Throughout the course, try to remember that everything you learn in the language opens avenues to the culture, and every exposure to the culture will help you in your understanding and eventual mastery of the language.

Find fun ways of exploring the new culture. Try listening to music composed in that foreign land or going to movies in the language you are learning. If there are restaurants in your area that serve foods from the countries where your new language is spoken, go. If the servers there can and will speak their native language, invite a friend along for a foreign language evening.

If your school has a foreign language house for your language, see what is involved in joining. If there is no foreign language table for your language on campus, try to interest an instructor in helping you start one. Spending a mealtime even once a week speaking your new language and hearing it spoken will help you learn and enjoy it, and you will likely meet other students as enthusiastic about using their new language skills as you are.

Try always to talk to your language instructors in the new language, even when you meet them outside of class. Try to get to know native speakers of the language, and use your new language skills to talk with them. Ask them to tell you something about the place they come from. You will get valuable practice in listening comprehension as well as interesting, firsthand cultural information.

Investigate possibilities for study abroad. If a year or semester program is not an option for you, perhaps a summer study trip is. Even an intensive summer school session at home or an "immersion" weekend is better than getting no exposure outside your regular classes. Talk to students in advanced courses about what they have done to supplement their regular classwork; get recommendations from your instructor or other members of the language department.

The point is to find as many ways as possible to fill in the gaps that typically appear when adults try to learn a new language. Also try to extend your knowledge of the language's culture. It may be harder in some ways for adults to learn languages; but adults also have a greater variety of means with which to attack the task than children do. Exploring those means is an important part of your job as an adult learner of a foreign language.

SUMMARY

How is learning a foreign language different from learning other subjects?	Learning a language entails learning both knowledge and skills. You have to learn "facts," but you also have to become proficient at using those facts. Furthermore, learning a language is not just one task; four distinct skills are involved.
What are the four language skills?	Listening, speaking, reading, and writing. Although these skills require some differences in approach, they also have characteristics in common. You must work on all four skills more or less simultaneously, throughout your language study.
Why do children often have an easier time learning languages than adults do?	Children are less inhibited about imitating what other people say—and imitation is an essential part of building new language habits. In addition, children do not have an established set of language habits that might interfere with the new ones they are trying to develop.
What advantages do adult learners have?	Adults have rational skills that children do not have. These skills enable adults to understand something about how language works. Adults can use this knowledge to speed up the imitation process that takes so long when people learn their first language.
Why is thinking not the most important part of learning a language?	Language is largely a set of habits, and you have to *do* things rather than just think about them in order to build those habits. Furthermore, languages do not always work in a logical way. Some things—the meanings of certain idioms, for instance—you simply have to memorize, repeating them until they become second nature. You cannot figure them out, no matter how hard you think about them.

Why is studying out loud important even on written assignments? Why is it a good idea to write out oral assignments?	Visual and auditory memory are enhanced dramatically when they are supplemented by motor memory. The more different kinds of memory you have working for you at any one time, the more likely you are to implant what you are learning in your long-term memory.
How are translating and reading different from each other?	Translating means reproducing in one language precisely what is said or written in another language. Reading entails thinking and understanding in the original language without using a second language as an aid. Hence translating necessarily involves at least two languages; reading involves only one.
Why is the time spent in class especially important in a language course?	In most language courses, the class hours are the closest you can get to an environment like the one in which the language you are learning is spoken. And when part of your learning is done by imitation, anything that helps create the right atmosphere is especially valuable.
How is culture connected to language study?	Language is in part a means of communicating culture—the ways people think and behave. When you learn the language, you are learning something about the culture. Conversely, learning something about the culture will probably make your language study more interesting, and it should help put what you are learning into perspective.

HAVE YOU MISSED SOMETHING?

Sentence Completion

Complete the following sentences with one of the three words or phrases listed below each sentence.

1. The most critical skill you need to master in learning a foreign language is learning _____ .

    the grammar   to listen   how to practice

2. You cannot construct _____ on the basis of rules.
   abstract ideas   cultural ideas   idiomatic expressions

3. By saying foreign words out loud, you are adding to your _____ .
   long-term memory   short-term memory   motor memory

Matching

In each blank space in the left column, write the letter preceding the phrase in the right column that matches the left item best.

_____ 1. Content

_____ 2. Culture

_____ 3. Motor

_____ 4. Imitation

_____ 5. Vocabulary

_____ 6. Idiom

a. A basic means of learning one's native language
b. The biggest challenge in reading a foreign language
c. Includes habits and customs as well as art
d. An expression peculiar to a particular language
e. Helpful in figuring out what a word means
f. The most efficient kind of memory

True-False

Write *T* beside the *true* statements and *F* beside the *false* statements.

_____ 1. Adults learn languages better than children because they are more mature.

_____ 2. Language involves at least four skills.

_____ 3. The same language skills are equally easy or hard for everyone.

_____ 4. Translating is a necessary part of reading.

_____ 5. Memorization is a critical part of language learning.

_____ 6. If you aren't tired when you leave a language class, you probably haven't worked hard enough.

_____ **7.** One trick in speaking a foreign language is to learn new sentences backward.

Multiple Choice

Choose the phrase that completes each of the following sentences most accurately, and circle the letter that precedes it.

1. Language study entails learning both facts and
a. vocabulary.
b. figures.
c. skills.
d. grammar.

2. Language study primarily involves development of a set of
a. habits.
b. words.
c. rules.
d. verbs.

3. The most difficult of the language skills is
a. listening.
b. speaking.
c. reading.
d. writing.

4. In foreign language study, the first rule of effective listening is
a. adjust!
b. believe!
c. question!
d. concentrate!

5. Making a new language second nature requires
a. repetition.
b. effort.
c. concentration.
d. all the above.

6. Unlike children, adults who learn a language can understand its
   a. meaning.
   b. structure.
   c. sentences.
   d. translations.

7. One good way to improve your reading skill in a foreign language is to
   a. look up every unfamiliar word as soon as you come to it.
   b. spend a long, uninterrupted block of time on one reading passage.
   c. look up unfamiliar words only if you still haven't figured out what
      they mean by the third time you encounter them.
   d. copy the whole passage into your notebook.

Short Answer

Supply a brief answer for each of the following items.

1. In what ways can you add to your knowledge of other cultures?

2. Explain why reading a foreign language is both easier and harder than
   listening and speaking.

3. What is the difference between translating and reading?

4. Discuss how embarrassment affects one's learning a new language.

5. Why is falling behind an especially big problem in language courses?

Vocabulary Building

Directions: Make a light check mark (✓) alongside one of the three words
(choices) that most nearly expresses the meaning of the italicized word in the
phrases that are in the left-hand column. Answers are given on p. 146.)

		1	**2**	**3**
1.	to *discriminate* sounds	differentiate	intermingle	harmonize
2.	in a *dialogue*	recitation	discussion	soliloquy
3.	*consolidate* your notes	preserve	separate	bring together
4.	*sophisticated* level	cultivated	provincial	uncomplicated
5.	maintain the *illusion*	existence	actuality	unreality
6.	*cumulative* nature	collective	dispersive	cloudy
7.	are *integrally* related	inherently	partially	peripherally
8.	a *prototype* bridge	lengthy	curved	model
9.	scientific *validity*	inaccuracy	weakness	soundness
10.	*suppress* its conclusions	repress	express	exceed
11.	research being *squelched*	exposed	encouraged	crushed
12.	*insidious* problem	conspicuous	treacherous	harmless
13.	quota *infidelity*	observance	faithfulness	nonadherence
14.	tax *incentives*	laws	motivations	dissuasions
15.	a *coalition* of parties	alliance	separation	conflict
16.	*contentious* issues	compatible	congenial	controversial
17.	*adamantly* refused	firmly	meekly	loudly
18.	this *repudiation*	reputation	approval	rejection
19.	*deterring* capitalists	hindering	encouraging	pursuing
20.	*pompous* politicians	obese	arrogant	inglorious
21.	*exotic* fruit	foreign	indigenous	ordinary
22.	undue *harriedness*	distress	comfort	haste
23.	company *heralded*	studied	announced	kept secret
24.	big *acquisitions*	procurements	deprivations	relinquishments
25.	*encompassing* an area	containing	omitting	measuring

Additional Multiple-Choice Questions

1. It's normal for people learning a foreign language to
   a. have difficulty with their first language.
   b. get their language habits mixed up a bit at first.
   c. excel at linguistics.
   d. have trouble with reasoning tasks.

2. Learning to listen to a foreign language comes down to a matter of learning to
   a. speak.
   b. mimic sounds.
   c. discriminate sounds.
   d. adjust to repetition.

3. The most important thing to do in listening to a foreign language is to
   a. concentrate.
   b. reflect.
   c. recite.
   d. interpret.

4. *Global understanding* means that your understanding is
   a. worldly.
   b. specific.
   c. exact.
   d. general.

5. Language is a set of
   a. characters.
   b. modes.
   c. habits.
   d. mysteries.

6. *Frequent reentry* of material in learning to speak a foreign language refers to
   a. substitution of words.
   b. a grammatical device.
   c. thinking at frequent intervals of material already learned.
   d. the language of your childhood.

7. You learn to read in a foreign language so that you can avoid having to
   a. translate.
   b. study.
   c. remember.
   d. use the dictionary.

8. Probably the most difficult skill to master in a foreign language is that of
   a. reading.
   b. speaking.
   c. listening.
   d. writing.

9. Learning a foreign language is a task best accomplished by having
   a. large doses infrequently repeated.
   b. small doses frequently repeated.
   c. large doses frequently repeated.
   d. small doses infrequently repeated.

10. One of the most satisfying aspects of learning a foreign language
is that it
a. lets you speak at foreign language tables.
b. satisfies your foreign language requirement.
c. allows you access to a different culture.
d. is useful on your resumé.

ANSWERS FOR STUDYING FOREIGN LANGUAGES

Sentence Completion

1. to listen   2. idiomatic expressions   3. motor memory

Matching

1. e   2. c   3. f   4. a   5. b   6. d

True-False

1. F   2. T   3. F   4. T   5. T   6. T   7. T

Multiple Choice

1. c   2. a   3. d   4. d   5. d   6. b   7. c

Vocabulary Building

1. 1   2. 2   3. 3   4. 1   5. 3   6. 1   7. 1   8. 3   9. 3   10. 1   11. 3   12. 2   13. 3
14. 2   15. 1   16. 3   17. 1   18. 3   19. 1   20. 2   21. 1   22. 1   23. 2   24. 1
25. 1

Additional Multiple-Choice Questions

1. b   2. c   3. a   4. d   5. c   6. c   7. a   8. d   9. b   10. c

There are two worlds: the world that we can measure with line and rule, and the world we feel with our hearts and imagination.

LEIGH HUNT

(1784–1859), British writer and editor of the Examiner

D

Supplementary Chapter D

STUDYING LITERATURE

Textbooks aren't literature and literature isn't text—few people would dispute that. So why read *Sons and Lovers* as though it were *Statistics and Logic*? Each of the two types of writing marches to the beat of a different drummer. This chapter deals with

- What to look for in literature

- The EVOKER system for reading imaginative prose

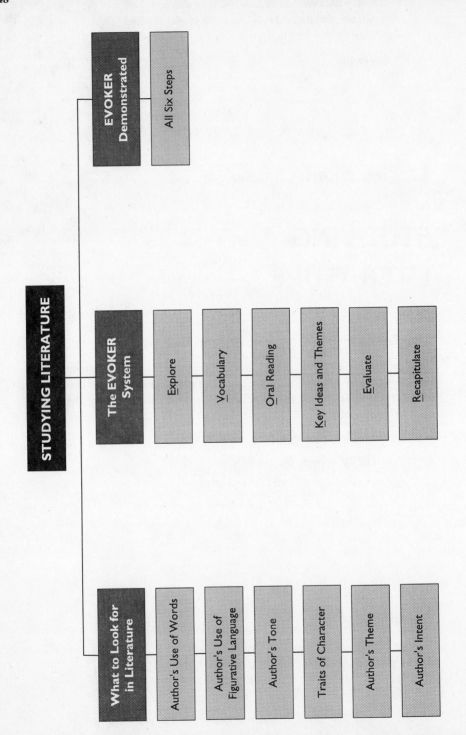

Reading literature (imaginative prose) is very much like looking at a painting. Neither reader nor viewer will learn much if he or she doesn't know what to look for.

WHAT TO LOOK FOR IN LITERATURE

As you read literature, notice how the author uses words, figurative language, tone, and characters to present his or her stories, ideas, and themes.

Author's Use of Words

Observe closely the way an author uses words to make a story interesting. The author may want to achieve a certain effect by choosing and arranging words in a particular way, perhaps to create a vivid picture or image, or to emphasize a point with a simple or complex sentence. For example, your idea of a person could be far different depending on whether the author says the man is *fat* or *stout, remarkable* or *odd, different* or *eccentric* and whether he *walks* or *struts*. Words also help to reveal an author's style. In sum, when you understand *what* an author does with words, and *how* the author does it, your enjoyment of the writing is bound to increase.

Author's Use of Figurative Language

Figures of speech are words used in an imaginative sense to emphasize or clarify statements that otherwise would be difficult to visualize and remember. For example, "The bargain-hungry shoppers charged into the store like a herd of elephants" stirs the imagination. You can visualize the action better than if the writer had said, "The shoppers entered noisily."

Author's Tone

Sometimes words *say* one thing but *mean* another. To find out what a writer is saying, you must know whether the writer is being serious, satiric, sarcastic, ironic, or playful. In many instances, if you miss the tone, you'll miss the intent. A classic example of a piece of writing that means something quite different from what it says is Jonathan Swift's essay, "A Modest Proposal." Written in 1729, the "proposal" suggested that the desperate situation of the Irish people could be remedied by promoting a project for butchering and marketing surplus children as delicacies for the table, "very proper for landlords, who, as they have already devoured most of the parents, seem to have the best titles to the children." To take the essay literally, as a hideous and inhuman proposal, is of course to miss the entire point: Swift's savage indignation on behalf of the Irish people, his hatred of injustice and inhumanity. Understanding that the tone is bitterly satiric, we can appreciate this essay as a great humane statement intended to shock readers into awareness of an intolerable condition.

How do you know when to take a selection literally? There is no definite and easy way to tell. But you will acquire sensitivity to attitude, intent, and tone through reading and analyzing. Start with examples identified for you as satirical, ironic, humorous, and so on, and look for words and phrases that provide clues. With practice, you will develop an alert sense for what an author means beyond what he or she says.

Traits of Character

Authors want their characters to be identified as real people rather than as storybook types or caricatures. Most authors create characters gradually, attributing to them a wide range of thoughts, emotions, and actions. From these materials, you build the characters in your own mind. To distinguish one character from another on the basis of traits such as pride, jealousy, shrewdness, and snobbishness, you should watch for the distinctive words and actions of each character.

Author's Theme

Most enduring literature presents a theme or series of themes. Through their stories and characters, authors tell you what they believe and how they feel about life, humankind, truth, morality, hypocrisy, tolerance, suffering, death, love—issues of central concern to us all. In works of imaginative literature, you can see and perhaps better understand human motivation and behavior and their consequences.

Author's Intent

As you read, keep in mind these two questions: "Why did the author write this story?" and "What did he or she try to accomplish?" Considering these questions can lead you to see the author's purpose for writing the story you're reading, which in turn can further your understanding of the story's content, meaning, and implications.

THE EVOKER SYSTEM

A systematic approach to reading a novel takes some of the guesswork out of reading and lays a firm foundation for your continued development in reading and thinking. The EVOKER system provides you with a step-by-step procedure for approaching a piece of imaginative prose. The name is a mnemonic for Explore, Vocabulary, Oral Reading, Key Ideas and Themes, Evaluate, and Recapitulate. The steps are as follows:

1. Explore: Read silently and quickly through the entire selection without stopping to reread a portion that you perhaps did not fully understand. By pressing on, you will frequently clarify some obscure points. And by reading the entire selection without stopping, you will gain a feeling for the whole.
2. Vocabulary: Do not stop to look up unfamiliar words: by continuing to read, you may come across a familiar synonym. Instead, as you read, quickly underline any word that is not entirely clear to you. After you have finished the selection, look up in the dictionary definitions of words whose meanings are still vague. As you discover the meaning of each word, fit it into the context by rereading the entire paragraph in which it appears. By doing so, you will preserve the unity of the paragraph.
3. Oral Reading: Look over the selection a second time, reading portions aloud using proper intonation (expression). Hearing not only aids comprehension but also communicates to you the stress, rhythm, and power of words and word sequences.
4. Key Ideas and Themes: During both the silent and the oral reading in the previous two steps, you will have perceived and approximately located various key ideas. Now, in this step, locate these key ideas more precisely and underline them. This procedure will help make the key ideas stand out so you can better see and understand the author's plan of organization. The sum of these key ideas should help you formulate a general analysis of the author's main and subsidiary themes.
5. Evaluate: Evaluate, in context, the key words, figurative language, and ideas to see how they contribute to the theme or themes. Notice, too, how the key words develop the shades of meaning, the mood, and the tone of the selection. This detailed analysis extracts the fullest meaning of every important word, phrase, and sentence.

6. Recapitulate: Having completed all these steps, you are now ready, like someone who has just fitted the last piece of a jigsaw puzzle in place, to draw back and look at the whole picture—to read the entire selection or episode slowly and completely, with insight and understanding.

EVOKER Demonstrated[1]

The following excerpt is from D. H. Lawrence's *Sons and Lovers*, which is often assigned in English courses. Notice how each of the six steps is applied to the two short paragraphs; notice, too, how much information is gained from these fifty-two words.[2] When you are preparing to discuss an assigned novel or short story in class, this is the way to prepare for it.

> Before the younger man knew where he was he was staggering backwards from a blow across the face.
> The whole night went black. He tore off his overcoat and coat, dodging a blow, and flung the garments over Dawes. The latter swore savagely. Morel, in his shirtsleeves, was now alert and furious.

Now, to apply the close-reading system—The EVOKER—to the above passage, we take the following steps:

First, we read the passage silently.

Second, we make sure that all words are correctly understood. For instance, we might look up the word *staggering* to understand its full meaning.

Third, in the oral reading of the selection we unmistakably pick up the hissing sound made by the *s*'s in "swore savagely."

Fourth, we look for the author's theme or intention. In this selection the important aspect is the author's intention—to describe, in detail, a fight between two men. Next, we look for the organizational pattern—specifically, in order to find and mark off the steps taken by the author to achieve his purpose. The main steps or divisions are as follows: The author plunges the reader into the action—two men fighting; then the author describes the setting while keeping the fighting active—the time is night; next, he gives a physical description of the men; and, finally, he describes the mental states of both men.

Fifth, by using the technique of detailed analysis to differentiate among shades of meaning, we find the following:

[1]"Two Systems for Comprehending Literature." Reprinted by permission of The College Reading Association.
[2]"Reading Imaginative Prose: The EVOKER System." Reprinted by permission of The College Reading Association.

The first sentence reveals that the younger man received an unexpected blow from the older man. We know that the blow was a hard one because the word *staggered* was used. Here *staggered* means the movement of legs not only to keep one's balance but also to keep from sinking to the ground because of the physical shock of the blow affecting the senses.

In the second sentence the author tells much with only a few words. The word *black* reveals to us not only that it is night but also that the blow to the younger man was almost a knockout.

The third sentence supplies information that helps the reader fill in the physical details more completely; at the same time, the words *overcoat* and *coat* indicate that it is quite cold.

Then, with the phrase *dodging a blow*, the author realistically keeps the fighting going while telling about the coats. In the same sentence, the words *flung the garments over Dawes* indicate that the fight is a serious one—to the finish. (In a gentlemen's fight the men would have carefully placed their coats aside with the intention of putting them on after they had gone through the motions of saving "honor.")

In the fourth sentence the word *savagely* connotes a beastlike frame of mind. We perhaps get a picture of a man who is almost fully possessed by the basic instinct of "kill or be killed." In addition to supplying the reader with a sense of Dawes's mental state, the word *savagely* conjures up the physical picture of a brutelike hulk of a man.

In the fifth sentence the author completes the picture of how Morel looks after discarding his coats but more important are the words *alert* and *furious*. The word *furious* implies a man who is geared up for a death struggle. And the word *alert* has, in this case, both a mental and physical dimension. Morel is alert physically, ready to act or react—not, however, with blind and savage instinct but under the dictates of the mind. The mind still has control over the body.

The sixth, and last, step of the EVOKER system is the recapitulation. Having used the detailed analysis to extract the fullest meaning from every word, phrase, and sentence, and now that each individual episode has been seen in the reader's mind and has contributed its bit, the reader is ready to read the entire story slowly and completely, with insight and understanding.

The EVOKER system will help you look for specific details in literature and to be fully aware of what you find. Once awareness becomes habitual, you will realize that a printed page yields up its meaning not to the eyes but, rather, to the mind, which reads and rereads, puzzles and ponders, quizzes and questions, recalls and recites, reflects and recapitulates.

SUMMARY

How does the author's use of words affect the meaning of his or her writing?

Authors choose their words carefully to ensure that they convey exact shades of meaning and emphasis. The words *skinny* and *svelte*, for example, may be considered synonyms, but their effect on the reader can be entirely different. Your job as reader is to determine the author's purpose behind his or her word choice.

What is the big question you should ask when you read literature?

A good basis for reading any work of literature is the question "Why did the author write this story?" When you begin to understand the author's primary intent, then you will gradually see the reasons for his or her choice of words, characters, and plot.

Why was the EVOKER system devised?

The EVOKER system was designed to give you a procedure for comprehending and evaluating a piece of literature.

In reading literature, isn't it best to look up new words as you encounter them?

No. It is vital that you preserve the unity of each paragraph as you read literature. Unfamiliar words are often defined through context as you read on. If not, you can look them up in the dictionary after your first, uninterrupted reading.

What is the purpose of reading a passage aloud?

Oral reading adds another dimension to your understanding of literature. There is no better way to appreciate the rhythm, emphasis, and sonority of literature than by reading it aloud.

What is the value of locating a passage's key ideas?

Understanding the overall intent of an author's work is like doing a jigsaw puzzle. In this case, the key ideas are the individual pieces. As is not the case with a standard puzzle, however, you have to locate the pieces before you can use them. Once you find the key ideas, you can fit them together into the big picture—the author's intent or theme.

HAVE YOU MISSED SOMETHING?

Sentence Completion

Complete the following sentences with one of the three words or phrases listed below each sentence.

1. Authors want their characters identified as _____ .
   storybook types   real people   extreme personalities

2. The tone of a selection is developed by _____ .
   key words   actions of characters   physical setting

3. The purpose of the EVOKER system is to foster _____ .
   enjoyment   awareness   experimentation

Matching

In each blank space in the left column, write the letter preceding the phrase in the right column that matches the left item best.

_____ 1. Explore

_____ 2. Vocabulary

_____ 3. Oral reading

_____ 4. Key ideas

_____ 5. Evaluate

_____ 6. Recapitulate

a. Use intonation to help comprehension
b. Draw back and look at the whole picture
c. Do it quickly and without stopping
d. Use content as a powerful tool
e. Underline any that you have ascertained
f. Mark it now but look it up later

True-False

Write *T* beside the *true* statements and *F* beside the *false* statements.

_____ 1. The meaning of a printed page is immediately apparent.

_____ 2. In literature, words say what they mean.

_____ **3.** Figures of speech can help clarify a hard-to-remember statement.

_____ **4.** You can't always be sure whether to take a passage literally.

_____ **5.** The EVOKER name is a mnemonic device.

Multiple Choice

Choose the phrase that completes each of the following sentences most accurately, and circle the letter that precedes it.

1. Reading literature is like examining a
    a. painting.
    b. patient.
    c. prism.
    d. plant.

2. An author's choice of words helps to reveal his or her
    a. style.
    b. contemporaries.
    c. intelligence.
    d. research.

3. Figures of speech can make a statement easier to
    a. visualize.
    b. understand.
    c. remember.
    d. do all the above.

4. Missing a passage's tone can mean missing
    a. its rhythm.
    b. its intent.
    c. its punctuation.
    d. none of the above.

5. Most enduring literature has at least one
   a. satirical idea.
   b. theme.
   c. conclusion.
   d. dialogue.

6. During your first reading of a selection, unknown words should be
   a. underlined.
   b. looked up in a dictionary.
   c. skipped over.
   d. pronounced out loud.

7. Literature yields its deeper meaning to the
   a. eyes.
   b. inquisitive mind.
   c. author alone.
   d. patient.

Short Answer

Supply a brief answer for each of the following items.

1. How do you decide whether a writing selection should be taken literally?

2. Why is a theme so important in an author's work?

3. What is the value of EVOKER's Recapitulate step?

4. Distinguish between an author's *tone* and an author's *intent*.

Vocabulary Building

Directions: Make a light check mark (✓) alongside one of the three words (choices) that most nearly expresses the meaning of the italicized word in the phrases that are in the left-hand column. (Answers are given on page 160.)

		1	**2**	**3**
1.	*intolerable* condition	unendurable	reasonable	neutral
2.	take a selection *literally*	carelessly	figuratively	face value
3.	identified as *satirical*	reality	ironical	theoretical
4.	book types or *caricatures*	exaggerations	characters	types
5.	*obscure* points	prominent	apparent	unclear
6.	*dissident* shareholders	dissatisfied	similar	conforming
7.	*arcane* business	understood	open	mystical
8.	dissidents truly *mollified*	appeased	agitated	neutralized
9.	strange genetic *mutation*	outcome	change	progression
10.	*insidious* personality changes	obvious	shady	honest
11.	it looks *haphazard*	deliberate	intentional	disorderly
12.	at a *staid* pace	jaunty	dignified	playful
13.	with astonishing *alacrity*	reluctance	nimbleness	unconcern
14.	conservative and *insular*	narrow	liberal	wordly
15.	an *entrepreneurial* company	traditional	established	start-up
16.	it will be *relentless*	stern	compromising	compassionate
17.	the more *viable* tool	vivid	thoughtful	workable
18.	the *cadre* of directors	group	quality	experience
19.	*complementing* their businesses	recognizing	applauding	dovetailing
20.	many *culinary* classes	fashion	cooking	crafts
21.	traveling to *exotic* places	native	foreign	commercial
22.	spreading *skepticism*	neutralism	disbelief	faith
23.	such an *innovation*	theory	improvement	practice
24.	ending the *gridlock*	compromise	antagonism	jam
25.	an *audacious* claim	daring	cautious	amiable

Additional Multiple-Choice Questions

1. An author's word choice helps reveal his or her
    a. history.
    b. plot.
    c. style.
    d. status.

2. Understanding *what* an author does with words and *how* the author does it will
    a. take the magic out of most stories.
    b. increase your enjoyment in reading.
    c. reveal the plot right from the start.
    d. make you superior to him or her.

3. Figures of speech are used to
   a. emphasize and clarify.
   b. criticize and vilify.
   c. outline and identify.
   d. decrease and pacify.

4. If you fail to pick up on an author's tone, you also risk missing his or her
   a. defense.
   b. control.
   c. advice.
   d. intent.

5. Swift's "A Modest Proposal" is a classic example of prose that is
   a. literal.
   b. satirical.
   c. unethical.
   d. serious.

6. Most enduring literature has some sort of
   a. motif.
   b. hypocrisy.
   c. theme.
   d. love.

7. The first <u>E</u> in the EVOKER mnemonic asks you to
   a. Explain.
   b. Explore.
   c. Evaluate.
   d. Evolve.

8. With the EVOKER system, the passage is read
   a. silently.
   b. aloud.
   c. two times.
   d. three times.

9. The Key Ideas direction in the EVOKER system calls for a
   a. detailed analysis.
   b. general analysis.
   c. brief recapitulation.
   d. brief exploration.

10.   A detailed analysis often reveals the passage's
      a.   organizational patterns.
      b.   typographical errors.
      c.   themes or intentions.
      d.   shades of meaning.

ANSWERS FOR STUDYING LITERATURE

Sentence Completion

1. real people   2. key words   3. awareness

Matching

1. c   2. f   3. a   4. e   5. d   6. b

True-False

1. F   2. F   3. T   4. T   5. T

Multiple Choice

1. a   2. a   3. d   4. b   5. b   6. a   7. b

Vocabulary Building

1. 1   2. 3   3. 2   4. 1   5. 3   6. 1   7. 3   8. 1   9. 2   10. 2   11. 3   12. 2   13. 2
14. 1   15. 3   16. 1   17. 3   18. 1   19. 3   20. 2   21. 2   22. 2   23. 2   24. 3
25. 1

Additional Multiple Choice Questions

1. c   2. b   3. a   4. d   5. b   6. c   7. b   8. d   9. b   10. d

Part Four

USING THE "ROUNDTABLE DISCUSSIONS" VIDEOTAPES

INTRODUCTION

The "Roundtable Discussions" videotapes were created for use in any course on study skills and techniques for success in college. *Study Strategies* covers the four primary proficiencies (note taking, reading, memory, and test taking) and introduces specific tools and techniques for mastering each set of skills. The *Life Skills* videotape addresses three areas that help to ensure success (goal setting, time management, and stress management).

   This supplement is intended to help you integrate the *Study Strategies* and *Life Skills* videotapes with the textbook and other materials you use. In addition, you will find suggested activities and summary exercises for linking specific topics with students' experiences both inside and outside the classroom.

   For information on ordering the "Roundtable Discussions" videotapes, please contact your Houghton Mifflin representative or telephone 1-800-733-1717.

SUGGESTED USE OF VIDEOTAPES

The "Roundtable Discussions" videotapes are structured according to major tasks and their logically related skills. For example, Segment One focuses on taking notes in class along with active listening and on taking notes while studying along with the Cornell method. Understanding this approach may be helpful as you integrate the video segments and activities with your textbook material and exercises.

In general, each videotape segment presents "the task" as a challenge for one of the students and "the skills, tools, and techniques" as helpful solutions that work for his or her friends. This approach is designed to introduce each challenge area in a context that will

- show students the actions that can be taken to deal with the challenge.

- show students that they probably already have many of the skills needed to succeed.

- stimulate students to identify their own challenges and begin to formulate ways of improving.

- motivate students to develop a personal approach to effective learning.

The sequence in which you use the video segments will depend upon the structure of your course and the ability level of your students. In most instances, you will probably want to play a specific video segment through as an introduction to the topic at hand, then replay appropriate portions of that segment as you address particular tools or techniques. Before showing each segment of the videotape, you may decide to conduct a brief discussion or self-assessment of your students' current attitudes, habits, and difficulties relating to the particular topic.

Part One presents a segment-by-segment description of the videotape contents and suggests classroom activities to help you link the videotape with your existing curriculum. In Part Two, you will find a summary exercise for each segment. These exercises are designed to demonstrate to students the practical value of the skills presented, not just in the classroom but also in many aspects of personal, academic, and professional life.

PART ONE: SEGMENT ACTIVITIES

Tape One—Study Strategies, Segment One: Note Taking

This segment of the videotape introduces the skills required for effective note taking and specifically addresses active listening, deciding what is important, mind mapping, and the Cornell method of note taking. Students' note-taking skills can be measured by how well they are able to answer the questions provided below.

Active Listening

1. In the videotape, Pham has trouble taking notes in class. What do his friends mention as the possible sources of his problems?
2. List the five elements of active listening.
3. Which of these elements might you be able to control?
4. Identify all the factors that might hinder your ability to listen actively.
5. For each of these hindrances, identify how you might eliminate it or otherwise neutralize it so as to enhance your ability to listen actively.

Deciding What Is Important

In the videotape, one of the first suggestions Maria makes to Pham is that he has to *decide* to listen. Pham accepts her suggestion, but he still feels frustrated by his difficulty in evaluating the importance of what he is hearing.

1. What ideas do Pham's friends offer for deciding what is important?
2. List the cues identified in the video, and provide examples of each.
3. What other indicators is Pham told to look for?
4. Identify any ways (not mentioned in the video) you have of deciding what's important in a lecture.

Mind Mapping

Beverly shows Pham how to use mind mapping as a way to capture a lot of information quickly and succinctly.

1. Select a hobby, sport, or other activity you are especially good at or know a lot about.
2. Write a summary (of no more than one page) of the information you know about the activity, providing enough information for someone new to the activity to get started.

3. Draw an information or concept map of the activity.

4. Compare your narrative summary and mind map. How are they different? How are they alike?

Extended Activity: Ask several students to give short oral presentations on the hobby or sport they selected in the previous activity. Have the rest of the class draw concept maps while they are listening to the presentation. Then compare the maps drawn by the class with the one drawn by the presenter.

The Cornell Method

In the videotape, the last suggestion Pham's friends make is that he should have a note-taking system. Maria demonstrates the Cornell method.

1. On a blank sheet of paper, show the Cornell method for taking notes and indicate the purpose of each component.

2. Describe the steps for studying notes taken by using the Cornell method.

3. List the aspects of the Cornell method that are part of the note-taking system you currently use.

4. Identify aspects of the Cornell method you are not currently using but that you think will enhance your note-taking skills.

Reminders To Students

• Be honest with yourself about why you might have difficulty concentrating in certain subject areas.

• Find new motivations and methods for staying focused even when your level of interest may be relatively low.

• Decide for yourself which note-taking methods work best for you. Create your own approach.

Segment Two: Reading

This segment of the videotape addresses students' reading-related difficulties and introduces skills and techniques needed to improve study efficiency and comprehension. Specifically, this segment focuses on improving concentration, active reading, and the SQ3R System.

Concentration

1. In the videotape, Beverly seems to have difficulty with the amount of reading required in her courses. Based on what you saw in the flashback

to her study session, identify the aspects of Beverly's study habits that hindered her ability to concentrate.

2. For each item you listed in #1, describe what Beverly could do differently that would improve her concentration.

3. Review the list you made in #1 and identify any items that also describe your study habits.

4. Identify any additional distractions to which you know you are susceptible.

5. For each item you identified, describe how you might change your approach for the better or otherwise deal with the distraction. (Be realistic about any limitations imposed by your particular situation.)

Active Reading

1. What suggestion does Pham offer Beverly for improving her reading skills?

2. List the six elements of active reading.

3. Review your notes to find the guidelines for "Deciding What's Important" that were introduced in the segment on note taking. Then create a new set of guidelines for active reading.

Extended Activity: To reinforce the idea that reading with a purpose makes a difference, have students survey the media for one week, making a note of each item (e.g., stories, editorials, and advertisements) connected to a topic you are currently studying.

SQ3R Reading System

1. In the videotape, Tina describes the SQ3R reading system she uses. Describe what "SQ3R" means and give a brief definition of each step in the process.

2. Select a chapter in a textbook (or some other multi-page passage) and read it according to whatever system you currently use.

3. Summarize for a partner what you read, providing as much detail as you can.

4. Select another chapter (or multi-page passage) and read it, using the SQ3R System.

5. Again, summarize for a partner what you read, giving as much detail as possible.

6. Compare the two reading methods in the following ways:
    a. Make sure you understand the material you read.
    b. Ask your partner to evaluate your ability to articulate what you read.

    c.   Identify the aspects of each system that were most helpful and effective for you.

    d.   Integrate the best of both methods to create your own reading system.

Extended Activity: To heighten students' awareness that some reading tasks are more difficult than others, ask them to find and bring to class examples of material that they find especially difficult. In class, conduct a discussion of the impact an author's writing skills (or lack thereof) have on the reader's ability to concentrate and learn. Then ask students for examples illustrating the points you've covered (e.g., convoluted writing style, lack of organization, or poor topic sentences).

Reminders To Students

- Always keep a dictionary at hand, and use it to clarify the meanings of words of which you are not absolutely sure.

- Practice silently paraphrasing each paragraph as you complete it to help stay focused and to confirm your understanding of the material.

- Keep a list of new concepts you want to remember from every reading session.

- When faced with a passage or concept you don't understand, "talk it out" with yourself or with a study partner.

Segment Three: Memory

This segment of the videotape introduces the memory process and presents techniques for strengthening memory.

Extended Activity: To show that *remembering is a choice,* select a series of numbers or a phrase and write it on the chalkboard (either before students arrive or at the beginning of class), but do not make any comment about what you have written. Begin class as you normally would and then introduce the videotape segment. When the videotape segment ends (again without comment or explanation), erase what was written on the chalkboard and move on to the first activity.

Memory Process

1. What are the stages of memory?
2. What are the different kinds of memory?
3. In the videotape, what tips do Maria's friends offer her for strengthening her ability to remember?
4. Can you remember what was written on the chalkboard at the beginning of class?
5. Why do you think you remember what was written there? Or why do you think you don't?
6. Do those numbers (or words) have some particular meaning for you?
7. Do you think you remember what was written because it was on the board?

Memory Techniques

1. Identify the memory techniques Maria's friends suggest in the videotape.
2. Identify any additional memory techniques you use or know about.
3. For each of the memory techniques you've identified, describe why and how you think it works. Give any examples of times you have used these techniques.

Extended Activity: To help students understand how memory operates, ask students to work (either individually or in small groups) to complete the following assignment. Adapt this activity to fit the level of computer literacy of your students.

1. Create a concept map on whatever topic you choose.
2. Think about the three types of human memory—sensory, short-term, and long-term—and show how human memory parallels a computer's operation.

With class participation, discuss similarities in how human memory and computer memory operate. Summarize the activity by pointing out that decisions are made moment by moment (not always consciously) about which information will be stored for future retrieval and that everyone can exert conscious control over remembering and recalling information. (The drawing shown on page 168 may be helpful as a discussion guide.)

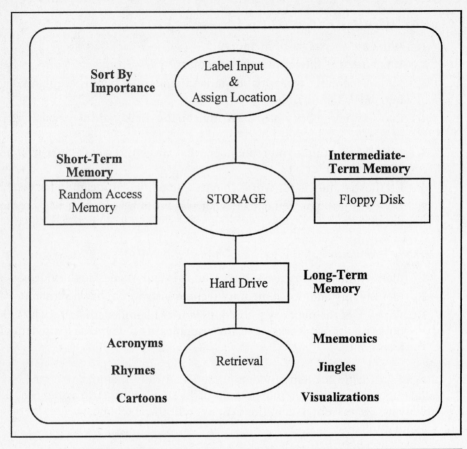

HOW MEMORY WORKS

Reminders To Students

- There are no "right" or "wrong" memory techniques—if something works for you, use it.

- Don't forget to choose to remember.

Segment Four: Test Taking

This segment of the videotape addresses test anxiety, test preparation, taking tests, and understanding different types of tests.

Test Anxiety

1. In the videotape, what kind of problems is Rob having in taking tests?
2. What solutions do his friends offer to help with each of these problem areas?
3. What are the most important factors in trying to cope with test anxiety?
4. Choose a situation in which you recall being anxious, and describe what happened to you (e.g., how you felt and what you were thinking at that time).
5. Looking back on that situation, can you identify some of the reasons behind your anxiety?
6. List some ways you might address each of those reasons in the future.

Test Preparation

1. Pham and the others offer some concrete suggestions to Rob about preparing for tests. List as many of those suggestions as you can remember.
2. Describe the system you use to prepare for tests.
3. Compare your current system with the suggestions given in the videotape, and then integrate the two to create a new system for yourself.
4. Evaluate your new test preparation system to see if it is realistic for you. If there are aspects you are not comfortable with, alter them to meet your individual needs.

Test Taking

1. List the test-taking strategies Rob's friends suggest.
2. List any additional strategies you have for taking tests.
3. Identify the aspect of test taking that is most difficult for you.
4. What are the reasons behind this difficulty?
5. How might you overcome this difficulty in the future?

Understanding Different Types of Tests

1. What guidelines for answering essay questions were given in the videotape?

2. Devise a system for remembering these guidelines, describe it in writing, and commit it to memory.

3. Using the guidelines, write an essay describing your personal history with taking tests. Include how you feel about taking tests, how well you generally perform on tests, the types of tests on which you perform well/poorly, the reasons behind your success or lack of success on that type of test, and any other issues related to the testing situation that you think are interesting or important.

4. When taking true-false tests, you should answer only those questions of which you are absolutely sure.   True _____   False _____

5. On true-false tests, you should choose true if only a small part of the statement is false.   True _____   False _____

6. You should always choose true unless you know the statement is false. True _____   False _____

7. Devise a method of remembering the guidelines for taking true-false tests, describe it in writing, and commit it to memory.

8. What system does Pham suggest to Rob for taking multiple-choice tests?

9. Devise a method of remembering how to approach multiple-choice tests, describe it in writing, and commit it to memory.

10. List the guidelines mentioned in the videotape for taking fill-in-the-blank tests.

11. List any additional guidelines or techniques you use on this type of test.

12. Devise a system for remembering these guidelines, describe it in writing, and commit it to memory.

Reminders To Students

• Mastery of a topic is the best reducer of test anxiety.

• You need a system for preparing yourself academically, physically, and emotionally to take tests.

• You need a system for taking each type of test.

• The best system is one that makes sense to you and that you create for yourself.

Tape Two—Life Skills, Segment One: Goal Setting

The purpose of this segment is to provide insight into how to set achievable goals, monitor progress toward them, and remain appropriately flexible in revising them over time. The presentation is structured around the idea that students can easily get sidetracked when they do not have clearly defined goals.

Long- and Short-Term Goals

1. In the videotape, Beverly seems to have lost her sense of direction. What advice do her friends offer her with regard to setting goals for the future?
2. What is Beverly's long-term goal?
3. What are Beverly's short-term goals?
4. Describe one of your personal long-term goals and the shorter-term goals toward attaining that goal.
5. Describe a long-term academic goal and the short-term goals required to reach it.

How to Write Effective Goals and Reach Them

1. List the criteria for writing effective goals that Beverly's friends mention in the videotape.
2. Look at each of the goals you wrote for yourself in #4 and #5 of the previous activity, and evaluate each against the criteria for effective goals. Rewrite your goals, if necessary.
3. What suggestions do Beverly's friends offer for ensuring that she reaches her goals?
4. Revisit your list of long- and short-term goals, and note the steps you can take to ensure that you reach them.

Extended Activity: Use the following process to push personal and academic goal setting to an even greater level of detail.

1. Identify goals that will take the longest amount of time to reach.
2. Work backwards in small steps to identify what must happen in order to achieve each goal.
3. For each short-term, intermediate, and long-term goal, identify any anticipated obstacles and ways to handle them.
4. Identify areas in which help is needed for realizing each goal.
5. Establish milestones for tracking progress and for revising plans, if necessary.

Reminders To Students

- Identify criteria for success in attaining your goals.

- Sharing your goals with someone and committing to a progress review will help you stay focused on your plan.

Segment Two: Time Management

This segment of the videotape provides ideas for analyzing how you spend your time, how to schedule time effectively, and how to cope with the urge to procrastinate.

Analyzing How You Spend Your Time

1. What guidelines do Tina's friends suggest for analyzing her time?
2. Draw a pie chart that reflects how you currently spend your time.
3. Is your allocation of time to each aspect of your life appropriate, given your current goals and needs? If not, draw another chart that reflects a more appropriate time allocation.
4. List everything you have to do tomorrow—from the time you get up until the time you go to sleep—and estimate how long you think each task will take. Then, as you go through the day tomorrow, record the actual time you spend on each task. Be sure to note all the departures from your planned schedule and the time actually spent.
5. Examine your list for discrepancies between the amount of time you estimated for each task and the actual time required. Did you over- or underestimate how long the task would take?
6. Examine your list and identify ways you might have used your time more efficiently.

Scheduling

1. Map out your schedule for tomorrow, showing every moment from getting up to going to sleep.
2. List all of the tasks that you need or want to accomplish, and estimate how much time each task will take.
3. Draw a new plan for your day, concentrating on making optimal use of your time.
4. Highlight any free time you may have available tomorrow, and think of a task you have planned for the following day that can be done in that amount of time.

Extended Activity: Once you have identified how you are currently spending your time and the tasks to be accomplished, use the following sequence to help you spend your time most appropriately.

1. Assign a priority to each of your goals or tasks by assessing both its urgency and its value to you. Devise a scale such as the one below that helps you evaluate your priorities.

    1 = most important; must be accomplished immediately (or first); biggest payback
    3 = important, but can be postponed; dependent on accomplishment of other goal
    5 = not very important; can be put off indefinitely with no real consequence

2. Review your current schedule or plan for accomplishing your goals to see if the priorities you have assigned are appropriate.
3. Revise your schedule according to your priorities.

Beating Procrastination

1. What strategies are given in the videotape for overcoming procrastination?
2. List the six ways given to beat procrastination.
3. Can you suggest any additional ways to beat procrastination?
4. Develop a device that will help you remember these strategies for overcoming the urge to procrastinate.
5. Identify one thing in your life that you've been putting off, and create a plan for beating the urge to procrastinate any longer.

Reminders To Students

•   Be realistic when allowing time to accomplish tasks.

•   Watch for gaps in your schedule, and take advantage of opportunities to fill them.

•   Be alert to the urge to procrastinate—and beat it.

Segment Three: Stress Management

This segment of the videotape addresses the physical and mental effects of stress and offers techniques and suggestions for dealing with stressors.

Recognizing Stress

1. What mental symptoms of stress does Maria mention in the videotape?
2. What physical symptoms of stress does she mention?
3. Indicate (with a *) any of the symptoms you listed in #1 and #2 above that you currently have or have had in the past.
4. To the best of your ability, identify the sources of the stress behind each of the symptoms you marked on your list.

Stressbeaters

1. List as many of the stressbeaters that Rob's friends suggest to him as you can remember.
2. List any additional stressbeaters you use or know about.
3. Review the symptoms of stress you listed in #3 of the previous activity, and identify the stressbeaters you might employ for each.
4. Describe the relaxation technique you use most often, and explain why you think it works for you.

Extended Activity: Using your level of tendency to avoid situations and activities as a stress indicator, work through the following sequence as a way of helping you manage your stress.

1. List the first three things that come to mind as situations or activities you try to avoid.
2. Briefly describe the sources and the nature of the stress you experience.
3. Think about the importance of each stressor in the context of your whole life. Devise a scale such as the one below.

    1 = situation/activity is extremely stressful, and occurs frequently; is essential to my success/sense of well-being
    3 = situation/activity is stressful, but occurs only occasionally; is only moderately important to my success/sense of well-being
    5 = situation/activity is uncomfortable, but occurs rarely; is not important to my success/sense of well-being

4. For any stressor you rated a 1 or 2, create a plan that will either reduce the amount of stress you experience or allow you to manage the situation differently.

Reminders To Students

- The first step in handling any type of stress is recognizing the symptoms.
- Don't ignore stress; eliminate it.

PART TWO: SUMMARY ACTIVITIES

Tape 1—Study Strategies, Segment One: Note Taking

1. List the situations both inside and outside of college in which active listening skills are important. Explain why better listening skills are important in each situation. Identify ways you might practice listening skills for that situation.

2. Identify the types of *verbal cues* you look for in determining the importance of information, and give examples of each.

3. Identify the types of *nonverbal cues* you look for in determining the importance of information, and give examples of each.

4. Drawing on your everyday experience as a consumer of advertising in all media, identify some examples of verbal and nonverbal cues, and evaluate their effectiveness in communicating what is important.

Segment Two: Reading

1. Identify some situations (apart from college) that require strong reading skills.

2. For each situation identified, suggest an appropriate reading system by adapting what you have learned about reading for college.

3. Briefly describe your most enjoyable reading experience, telling what you read, when it was, where you were, what made the experience special or memorable, and any other information you think is important.

4. Describe your most unpleasant reading experience, giving the same kind of detail as you provided in #3.

5. What conclusions can you draw about yourself and your attitude about reading from the experiences you described in #3 and #4?

Segment Three: Memory

1. Define *sensory memory* in your own words and list three times you have used your sensory memory.

2. List all the situations, careers, or activities you can think of in which sensory memory is the primary ingredient for success.

3. Identify the memory techniques likely to be most useful for strengthening sensory memory.

4. List three examples of short-term memory.

5. Describe all of the situations, careers, or activities you can think of in which short-term memory is the primary ingredient for success.

6. Identify the memory techniques likely to be most useful for strengthening short-term memory.

7. List three examples of long-term memory.

8. Describe all of the situations, careers, or activities you can think of in which long-term memory is the primary ingredient for success.

9. Identify the memory techniques likely to be most useful for strengthening long-term memory.

Segment Four: Test Taking

1. Identify the one aspect of test taking that causes you the most anxiety, and briefly describe your plan for coping with it in the future.

2. List other anxiety-inducing areas in your life, identify the likely sources of the anxiety, and list some ideas for coping with it.

3. What is your greatest challenge in preparing for tests?

4. Identify other areas in your life where adequate preparation is critical to success, and outline your system of preparation for each. (If you currently do not have such a system, begin to develop one here.)

5. Drawing on what you have learned about how to take tests, identify other areas in your life where the same approach might be helpful.

Tape Two—Life Skills, Segment One: Goal Setting

1. Briefly describe your reasons for being in college.

2. If you have a "master plan" for finishing college, outline it below. If you don't, outline your current thinking about the courses you have already completed and those you plan to take. Then see if you can identify the direction in which you seem to be headed.

3. Describe who (or what) is behind your current decision making about school. Do you feel completely in control, or are you doing what you think others expect?

4. Make a list of the things you get most excited about, and briefly note why.

5. Make a list of the things you most dislike, dread, or feel negative about, and briefly note why.

6. Looking at the lists you created in #4 and #5 above, can you see any patterns that help to clarify who you are, what you are good at and enjoy, and what you do not enjoy?
7. To what extent do the patterns you identified above reflect the choices you are currently making about college, work, and life in general?
8. What changes, if any, do you need to make to create more consistency between your current direction and the goals that promise you the most satisfaction?

Segment Two: Time Management

Divide into groups for the following activity.

1. Ask for a volunteer to record the group's proceedings.
2. Take turns so that group members identify one task they have put off for too long, while the rest of the group agrees on a fitting reward and sets a deadline for its completion.
3. As a group, agree on a method of following up on the assigned deadlines and rewards.

If it is feasible, have copies of the proceedings made for each group member so that deadlines can be tracked by the entire group. Alternatively, you might set a date and time toward the end of the term to reconvene and to recognize those who have earned their rewards.

Segment Three: Stress Management

1. Create a profile of the way you personally deal with stress in different types of situations. For example, "When I have too much to do, my shoulders get tight and I have tension headaches." "When I have to cope with a big change," etc.
2. For each of the situations you listed, identify the likely sources of the stress producing your symptoms.
3. To what extent do you have the capacity to change or control each of the situations causing your stress?
4. To the extent that you do have control, identify what you might do to eliminate the stress.
5. For the situations in which you do not have control over the stressors, identify how you might manage your symptoms.

6. Is each situation one you can handle on your own, or do you need help?

7. If help is needed in a particular situation, identify the kind of help you need and where you might find it.